Most Pocket Books are available at special quantity discounts for bulk purchases for sales promotions, premiums or fund raising. Special books or book excerpts can also be created to fit specific needs.

For details write the office of the Vice President of Special Markets, Pocket Books, 1230 Avenue of the Americas, New York, New York 10020.

SUSAN LEE'S ABZs of ECONOMICS

Introduction by Leonard Silk

POCKET BOOKS

New York   London   Toronto   Sydney   Tokyo

ACKNOWLEDGMENTS

Thank you to those who read parts of the manuscript: Tim Ferguson, Robert Barro, Chris Byron, Jim Flanigan, and Shelly Zalaznick.

And gratitude to my editors at *Vogue* magazine, who were willing to take a chance on a column written by an economist; to my friends who exhibited deep and abiding faith: Susan Chace, Deirdre Rosenberg, Peter Martin, Christopher Norwood, Bob Wilson, Ina Finkel, John Nanney, Tatiana Pouschine, Del and Adelaide Hubbell; and to my editor, Elaine Pfefferblit, and my agent, Ginger Barber, who were nothing if not cheerful throughout.

But most of all, my thanks go to the two editors who taught me that thinking like an economist doesn't have to mean writing like one, Bob Bartley and Jim Michaels.

For my mother

POCKET BOOKS, a division of Simon & Schuster Inc., 1230 Avenue of the Americas, New York, N.Y. 10020

ISBN: 0-671-55712-2

First Pocket Books trade paperback printing June, 1988

10 9 8 7 6 5 4 3 2 1

POCKET and colophon are trademarks of Simon & Schuster Inc.

Printed in the U.S.A.

CONTENTS

5

INTRODUCTION

Susan Lee is one of a kind—a natural-born teacher, an irreverent and sassy comedienne (a menace to the pompous on the television talk shows and an eviscerator of party lines, whoever's party line it might be), and a skillful economist with a mind and style of her own. Best of all, for the sake of the present business in hand, she writes well—lucidly and simply and gutsily. This kind of writing stems not just from knowledge and technical skill but from a genuine desire to reach her readers and help them.

Lord knows, the public needs all the help it can get if it is to understand what economics is all about. This is a science that cannot be walled off from other sciences or from the broad social environment. Economists themselves sometimes forget that or seek to so limit the terrain of economics as to exclude all considerations except the ones they want to focus on. In the old days, one of the favorite characters of the economics teacher was Robinson Crusoe, alone on his desert island, trying to decide how much of his labor to devote to gathering coconuts, how much to building a canoe that would enable him to catch more fish in the long run. A slight increase in the complexity of the environment occurred when Friday showed up, and the relations between capital and labor could be explored.

Actually, figuring out how Crusoe could best serve his own

welfare, with or without Friday, was complicated enough for some of the best minds in the early days of economics; and the result of their desert-island analysis still has relevance to the economics of teeming cities, national and international economies. For the simple Crusoe model clarified the choices an economic agent (whether an individual, a business, or a nation) needs to consider before deciding how best to serve his, her, or its welfare. That process of weighing and deciding what is in one's own best interest is what we mean by rational behavior. In fact, is human behavior rational? Economics usually assumes that it is, or ought to be. It would be difficult, perhaps impossible, to invent an economics of abnormal and irrational behavior. But, alas, that is not to say that a good deal of human behavior, even in the economic area, is not irrational—that is, likely to frustrate and defeat one's own purposes, hurt one's own well-being, and injure the interests of others, even those one does not want to hurt.

Human behavior—whether rational or irrational—is subject to many constraints. Some are technical, such as the "law of diminishing returns"—the more fertilizer you put on a given amount of land, the less extra output of wheat or corn you get from each extra dose of inputs. Whether you're sane or insane, whether you're Reagan or Qaddafi, that holds.

Some constraints are legal: You might increase your income, create a monopoly, and maximize your economic well-being by putting out contracts to have your competitors eliminated by gunmen, but the law says this is a no-no, and you might fry for it. All the same, it is sometimes done.

Some constraints are moral: Thou shalt not sexually harass thy employees, even if there is no law saying you can't; morality patrols an even vaster terrain than law but is an even more uncertain and subjective patrolman; consciences differ from person to person, and hypocrisy often vitiates proclaimed principles of morality, even when the principles are commonly held and asserted. It was the great French cynic, the Duc de La Rochefoucauld who said, "Hypocrisy is the tribute that vice pays to virtue."

But the greatest constraint on human behavior, as the mathematician John von Neumann and the economist Oskar Morgenstern, the creators of game theory, demonstrated, is the realization that what you want to do will cause other people to do something back to you. The sergeant on "Hill Street Blues" used to send the station's policemen and -women out with the injunction, "Do it to them before they do it to you." But the wiser and more exact message would be, "Before you do it to them, consider what they may do to you—and then consider what we may have to do, given all the factors, legal, political, social, financial, technical, and so on, that affect our behavior." Anybody who thinks I am overstating the complexities of police behavior has not, I suspect, had recent experience in trying to get the cops to deal with a burglary or some other crime.

So economics is a slice of life, not the whole of it, but a big bloody slice. It plays a crucial role in the everyday lives of individuals, businesses, and nations, and should help you cope better with life's daily trials and confusions. That's where Susan Lee's dictionary comes in. I think it can even help you win some of the games.

—LEONARD SILK

PREFACE

Interest in things economic seems to be everybody's dirty little secret. And few know that better than an economist. For several years of my life, for example, I had to answer the question, "What do you do?" by saying, "I teach economics." Despite the fact that my reply was always apologetic, the response was inevitable: eyes rolled, faces darkened, heads shook, and lectures on why economics was deficient, silly, or boring were given. Nonetheless, after all that came the question: "As an economist, what do you think of (fill in appropriate hot topic)?" The interest was as inevitable as the disapproval. The perfect dirty little secret.

At the risk of revealing myself as a pornographer, then, allow me to purvey my goods.

1. Interest in economics is natural. Everybody is an economic agent in some sort of economic system. Whether it's a consumer shopping for the lowest price or a seller looking for the highest bid, economics forces its way into lots of everyday decisions. It's hard to resist being curious about something so intrusive.

2. Interest in economics is desirable. Most everybody wants to make their money earn money. But being a good investor depends, in part, on knowing something about the economic climate. It's good to be interested in something you can profit by.

3. Interest in economics is important. Being a citizen of the world requires an intelligent rendering of the news. Knowing some economics is essential to a grasp of what's going on, who is doing what to whom, and why.

If all this is so, then why so much tut-tutting about economics (and pooh-poohing of economists)? Most obviously, economics is not always easy to figure. It is filled with lingo and buzzwords. Too, economics has gotten some bad press. There's that sobriquet, "the dismal science," and the fact that economists are endlessly disputing one another. In sum, it's easy to dismiss economics as a mug's game. Easy, but not smart.

And that's where this book comes in. The *ABZs* is a collection of the important buzzwords in economics. It does several things: provides a straightforward definition of the terms, an explanation of the ideas behind the terms, and, where appropriate, a glimpse into how the ideas fit into public policy debates.

The *ABZs* isn't meant to be read straight through. Nonetheless, if a question sends you to the page where inflation is explained, you might also have to turn to the page where deflation is described to get a more complete answer.

The *ABZs* won't turn you into an economist (and that's probably the last thing you want). But it can help you glide over some of the rough patches in your data base, help you make more sense of the daily headlines, and increase your understanding of why economic questions seem to pop up so often.

Absolute Advantage

A term beloved by international trade types. A country has an absolute advantage when it can produce something more efficiently than another country. Mexico, for example, has an absolute advantage over Canada in growing tomatoes. The possession of various absolute advantages makes trade among countries attractive. Why should Canada spend its resources producing tomatoes when lower-cost tomatoes can be had from Mexico?

Absolute advantage can apply also to firms or to individuals. And it makes good sense here, too: If one person makes delicious bread but is unable to hammer a nail deftly, then it's reasonable for that person to specialize in making bread and to purchase the services of a carpenter who can hammer nails. See COMPARATIVE ADVANTAGE.

Aggregate Demand

Simply the sum of all the separate demands in an economy for goods and services.

Aggregate demand is usually divided into four components:

One, the demand of households for goods and services. This is straightforward enough—households buy all sorts of things, from pork roasts to visits from the TV repairperson.

Two, the demand of firms and governments for investment goods. This can be anything from a hammer to a sophisticated computer.

Three, the demand of government for goods and services. Think of the government as a combo household-business: it needs a wide range of things, from flowers for the White House Rose Garden, secretarial services for Congresspeople, to complicated missiles for the Defense Department.

And four, the demand of foreign households, firms, and governments for goods and services. This can be anything from American designer jeans to American maritime insurance. See DEMAND.

Allocation of Resources

What every beginning textbook in economics says the science of economics is all about.

Resources are things like land, water, air, labor, machinery, and even technical know-how. These resources are said to be "scarce" in the sense that their availability is limited, although some resources are more limited than others. An economic system exists to distribute these resources, and an efficient economic system is one that allocates them best—that is, where resources are employed in producing the stuff that people want most and not in producing things that nobody wants.

At one extreme is a planned economy where state bureaucrats make the decisions to allocate resources. At the other extreme is a free market economy where prices determine the allocation. Most economies fall somewhere in between.

Antitrust

The "trust" part is a quaint way of describing monopolies, restraints of trade, or conspiracies to prevent competition. It refers to the turn-of-the-century practice of merging small companies into one huge one in order to limit supply and raise prices. (Most American history texts brim with colorful accounts of this activity—from the Railroad Trust and the Oil Trust to the Tobacco Trust.) The "anti" part signaled the end of the government practice of granting exclusive rights to one firm to carry on its business.

Antitrust laws made their appearance in the United States in 1889: The first major antitrust law was the Sherman Anti-Trust Act of 1890, which was followed by the Clayton Anti-Trust Act in 1914, the Robinson-Patman Act in 1936, and the Celler-Kefauver Amendment in 1956.

These laws cover all sorts of business activities that are thought to involve unfair forms of competition. Among the taboos are companies getting together to decide on a common price for their product (price-fixing), companies selling their products at varying prices in order to prevent competition in a certain market (price discrimination), companies pricing their products so low that potential competitors are discouraged from entering the market (predatory pricing), and certain types of mergers that might lead to one company dominating an industry. Firms found in violation of antitrust laws can find themselves compelled to pay rather stiff civil, and even criminal, penalties.

Some critics now contend that antitrust has gone too far. They have several reasonable arguments. First, monopolies aren't always bad—they often generate more rapid technological change and innovation than do firms that are busy competing with each other on a daily basis. Likewise, mergers that result in a firm dominating an industry often mean lower prices for consumers because the new, larger firm can produce more cheaply. Second, things aren't always as they seem —companies that appear to have a monopoly don't when the competition provided by foreign firms is included. Likewise, companies engaging in activities like price-cutting may be just aggressive competitors rather than potential monopolizers. And finally, critics can point to companies (like IBM) that have been prosecuted simply because they were "too big" rather than because they engaged in monopolistic activities, and to laws that were designed to protect small businesses but actually foster monopolistic situations.

Regardless of the economic or legal niceties, the fact remains that antitrust plaintiffs can make a pile of money if their lawsuits are successful. For example, a private firm that can prove damages from anticompetitive practices can sue for triple the losses actually suffered. So, too, the federal government has made a heavy-duty commitment to root out violators: the Antitrust Division of the Justice Department employs a slew of lawyers (and economists) to pursue alleged culprits with energy. And with fortitude—antitrust cases can take years before they even come to trial. See COMPETITION; MONOPOLY.

Appreciation

A rise in the price of a currency relative to other currencies. Under a system of floating exchange rates, the market sets the value of a currency—it's worth whatever buyers will pay for it. A nation with a "strong" currency—one that other nations wish to hold—will see its currency increase in value relative to other currencies. The nation with the appreciating currency usually then finds itself with a trade deficit because, as its exports become more expensive and its imports become less expensive, it imports more than it exports. See BALANCE OF PAYMENTS; FOREIGN EXCHANGE.

Arbitrage

A sophisticated version of buying cheap and selling dear. Arbitrage involves the act of buying something in one market and simultaneously selling it for more money in another market. Arbitraging is usually done by professional traders in the rarefied, high-tech world of foreign currency markets, or the spot market for commodities. But it can be accomplished anywhere and by anybody plucky—and lucky—enough to spot a favorable price discrepancy.

Opportunities for arbitrage are what bring prices in var-

ARBITRAGE

ious markets more or less in line with one another: when traders remove supply from cheap markets, they bring up prices there, and when traders deliver supply to expensive markets, they push down prices. Thus, arbitraging tends to equalize prices in all markets.

Asset

Can be either a physical or intangible property that has value to the owner. Individuals own assets in the form of houses or perfect credit records, firms own assets in the form of machines or copyrights. The asset's value lies in its use in providing future service or benefit: Homeowners can live in or sell their house; creditworthy individuals can borrow against their unblemished record.

The formal designation, "assets," is typically found on a firm's balance sheet. Here, assets are divided into "current" (either cash or things that can be readily turned into cash) and fixed (either buildings and equipment) or intangibles (copyrights, patents, and goodwill). Assets appear on one side of the balance sheet, liabilities on the other. See LIABILITY.

Austrian School

The roots of this school go deep into the nineteenth century with founder Karl Menger (1840–1921). Menger's chief contribution to economic thought lies in his exploration of the theory of value, particularly his notion that utility, or pleasure, declines with each extra unit of consumption. (Simple, really: The second consecutive banana split is not quite as good as the first.)

Today, however, the Austrian School is known by the work of two Menger disciples, Ludwig von Mises and Friedrich August von Hayek. Due to the work of these two men, the term "Austrian School" has become synonymous with laissez-faire capitalism.

Balance of Payments

A phrase used to describe the amount of money flowing in and out of a country.

The phrase itself is associated with some rather colorful images: from well-tailored international bankers flying about the world lending money to sleazy speculators "parking" money in various countries overnight. The reality, however, is rather less dramatic. Balance of payments involves a complex set of activities, including foreign exchange operations, which are mostly humdrum and always exceedingly difficult to grasp at one sitting.

For starters, the flows of investment money described above are only a small part of the world's payment transactions. Another—and a larger part of the U.S. balance of payments—involves flows of goods: exports of nuclear turbines or imports of wristwatches. These transactions are logged under the category called the current account. In addition to merchandise flows, the current account keeps track of exports and imports of services—transportation, travel, and financial and insurance services included. It also encompasses big chunks of government spending on military business and foreign aid, smaller chunks for Social Security recipients living abroad, and dividend and interest payments.

A second category, called the capital account, logs three types of flows. The long-term account consists of investments such as Japanese automobile factories in Ohio, American bank loans to Brazilian businesses, and transactions for stocks and bonds. The short-term account measures the investments known as "hot money" that zip from country to country in search of quick profits. And the official reserve account consists of the purchases and sales of gold and foreign currencies by the Federal Reserve Bank, and the dollars held by central banks of other countries. Unlike other transactions, activity in the official reserve account is not related to trading goods or services, making transfer payments, or investing. Rather, activity here "adjusts" the exchange rates among different currencies. And that brings the discussion around to the role of the foreign exchange markets in the balance of payments.

Simply put, foreign exchange markets are crucial to all this flowing about of goods and services because different countries have different currencies. If the Indian government wants to buy some nuclear turbines from a U.S. firm, it must first exchange its rupees for American dollars. Ditto for an American firm wishing to buy Japanese watches—dollars must be exchanged for yen. That seems very straightforward. And it will stay straightforward as long as countries import about as much as they export. But now consider what happens on the foreign exchange market when a country becomes a net importer; that is, when it buys more abroad than it sells, and thus runs a deficit in its balance of payments accounts.

Obviously, the importing country must exchange its money into foreign currencies in order to make its purchases. But because foreign countries are selling to the importing country rather than buying from it, they have little need for its currency. Since other countries don't want the importing country's currency, the value of its currency will decline, or depreciate, relative to other currencies. This effect holds in reverse, too: A country whose goods are in huge demand by other countries will find that its currency will appreciate compared to other currencies.

But the foreign exchange market is more than just an automatic adjustment mechanism among currencies. It is also made up of people who simply trade currencies, hoping to turn a profit by sudden moves in value. These traders watch a country's balance of payments as an early indicator of whether its currency will weaken or strengthen. Consider, for example, what happens when a country starts to run a deficit in its balance of payments. If traders rush to unload the hapless currency, its value will drop unless the central bank, using the resources in its official reserve account, steps in to buy its own currencies on the foreign exchange market. (This is called intervention in the exchange markets, and international types love to debate its usefulness in promoting something called stability.)

By now the intrepid might be wondering why all this back and forth, up and down, matters. The short answer is that it matters because countries are proud when their currencies are strong and embarrassed when they are weak. The long answer is that wide swings in a country's currency can upset trading relationships, causing grief to businesses in both the import and export sector. See FOREIGN EXCHANGE; GOLD STANDARD.

Balance Sheet

Document showing a firm's assets and liabilities at one particular point in time, usually the end of the year. It's called a balance sheet because assets equal liabilities; in fact, it's almost an arithmetical tautology.

Consider the balance sheet of a small firm, The Framistan Company: Assets, which consist of all the stuff Framistan owns, typically include the cash on hand, accounts receivable from framistans sold, inventories of both the materials to make framistans and the framistans made but not sold, and the factory and equipment needed to make framistans. Liabilities, which consist of all the stuff Framistan owes, typically include accounts payable to suppliers, salaries payable to workers, managers, and officers of the company, the mortgage on the factory, and, of course, any loans outstanding.

If The Framistan Company is a healthy enterprise, then its assets will add up to more than its liabilities. But that would unbalance the balance sheet. So the difference between assets and liabilities, called owners' equity (or net worth), is added to the liability side to make things equal. Why the liability side? Because owners' equity represents what is owned by the stockholders in The Framistan Company; thus, owners' equity is a liability—it is owed to the owners.

There is, however, one important element not reflected on Framistan's balance sheet—goodwill. This pleasant-sounding entry reflects Framistan's past success and future prospects: the high spirits of its employees, the utter respectability of its name, the good relationship it enjoys with its suppliers and customers. How does one put a price on goodwill? Simple. A buyer wishing to purchase The Framistan Company will probably have to pay much more than its owners' equity—that sum is then called goodwill.

The Framistan Company is a very stripped-down example. The balance sheet of a larger company, or one with fancy accountants, contains many more categories: Assets might include marketable securities and other investments; liabilities might include dividends payable and accrued taxes. And owners' equity might include preferred, common, and treasury stock, along with retained earnings.

Bank Failure

The polite way of designating a bankrupt bank. Banks are heavily regulated institutions—both their borrowing and lending practices are subject to scrutiny by state and federal agencies. Nonetheless, there are dozens and dozens of ways for a bank to get into serious trouble, from making a bunch of bad loans (not enough money coming in) to paying too high interest rates in order to attract deposit money (too much money going out). And, of course, a bank can also fail if its officers or staff engage in criminal mischief—like embezzling.

A bank is said to fail when it becomes insolvent; that is, when it doesn't have enough assets to cover its liabilities. But a failure can be an elusive event. Bank regulators have several options: They can prop up a technically failed bank by pumping in fresh money, as the Federal Reserve did in the case of Continental Illinois in 1984, or by issuing pieces of paper that banks can carry on their balance sheets as assets; or—and this is the preferred option—they can "merge" the failed bank with a healthy bank.

Before the 1930s, when bank regulatory agencies were put in place, a bank failure was a serious event. Back then, a failed bank was a failed bank—it closed its doors, leaving its depositors out in the cold, sometimes literally. Back then, even the rumor of a bank in trouble was enough to propel depositors there, and at other banks, into a rush to withdraw their funds. That, of course, only exacerbated the situation, so that healthy banks failed along with troubled ones. (This sequence of events was called a bank panic or a run on the banks.)

Nowadays, however, the existence of bank regulators and deposit insurance has made the handling of bank failures a fairly routine thing. These days, the only activity bank failures excite is editorials frothing and foaming about the irresponsibility (kind) or stupidity (not so kind) of bankers. See BANKING; FEDERAL RESERVE SYSTEM.

Bankruptcy

When an individual or corporation is legally declared insolvent by a court of law. A declaration of bankruptcy is more than just a statement, however. Insolvency doesn't (usually) describe a situation as mean as flat broke, but rather one in which liabilities are greater than assets. In other words, there are assets enough to pay back some, but not all, debts. And that's where bankruptcy proceedings come in.

Bankruptcy is actually a process by which the assets of the bankrupt are transferred to a court-appointed official. The official then liquidates the assets and makes sure that creditors with legal priority (the Internal Revenue Service, for example) get paid off before the rest of the creditors, and that the creditors are all treated fairly. Bankruptcy can be voluntary or involuntary. Individuals and corporations can declare themselves bankrupt, or creditors can get together and petition the court to declare a bankruptcy.

Banks and Banking

Commercial banks do many things: First and foremost, they provide a service called financial intermediation, and earn profits by doing so.

A description of modern banking can get a little tedious,

but it is not complicated. Consider, first, how banks provide financial intermediation in the economy. Despite its fancy term, this service involves nothing more than linking up people who want to save money with people who want to spend it. Savers place their money in banks, and banks, in turn, lend the money to spenders. Without financial intermediation, savings would rest idle under mattresses and borrowers would not be able to buy the goods and services that create jobs and make the economy go round. Quite clearly, financial intermediation is crucial for a healthy, sophisticated economy.

Banks provide intermediation by offering inducements for savers to put their money in bank accounts rather than under mattresses. That is, banks make it worth savers' while to become lenders.

For starters, banks provide a convenient and safe place to stash money. Customers deposit their money, or open an account and receive checks, which act as a substitute for cash. Sure, a bank account is not quite as handy as stuffing dough under a mattress, but for large purchases, using bank checks is safer and less awkward than cash. Banks also offer savers a rate of return (interest) on savings, making them a better deal than mattresses.

After luring savers into depositing their money, banks can transform savers into lenders by allowing borrowers to use the funds. Banks make borrowers pay for this privilege by charging interest on the money they lend. If all goes according to plan, banks pay savers less interest on deposits than they charge borrowers for loans. Banks use this "spread" to pay their expenses, and anything left over constitutes profit. In this respect, then, financial intermediation depends on banks being able to borrow cheap and lend dear.

Financial intermediation covers a lot of transactions. On the savers' side, it encompasses everything from modest, long-term passbook accounts to the immodest sums deposited overnight by large corporations. On the borrowers' side, it encompasses modest, short-term consumer loans to immodest, long-term loans to foreign governments.

But financial intermediation is not the only thing that banks do. They are also important players for the creation of money. While banks can't exactly print it—the way the federal government can—they do something almost as neat.

Consider, now, what happens when a saver makes a bank deposit. The amount of the deposit, itself, say $1000, appears on the bank's balance sheet as a liability; the bank owes the money to the depositor. However, the bank doesn't keep 100 percent cash against the deposit, but only a fraction of it: hence the bank reserves (say) 10 percent of the initial deposit in cash and lends out the rest. (Since loans are assets, the $1000 deposit liability will be balanced by $100 in cash and $900 in loan assets.) The bank makes the loan by opening an account from which the borrower may draw cash or write a check—it comes to the same thing. In other words, the bank has used the first depositor's account to *create* $900 of money in a second account.

But money creation doesn't stop there. Presumably, the borrower will withdraw money on the new account to pay for whatever it was he or she wished to borrow the money for. That money then usually goes into a third depositor's account. Again, the bank will reserve 10 percent of that deposit as $90 cash and lend the rest, $810, to another borrower. Presto, another $810 has been added to the supply of money. And so it goes, involving many depositors and their banks, until the created loan money becomes too small to measure. (In this example, the initial $1000 deposit can create $10,000 in new deposits—$9000 in the form of loans and $1000 as cash reserves.) The fractional reserve system, thus, allows banks to increase the money supply. See BANK FAILURE; FEDERAL RESERVE SYSTEM.

Barter

Obtaining goods or services without using money. Without using *money?* Sure. Money is a latecomer to the world of trading things. Primitive people satisfied their acquisition impulses by exchanging things like feathers for things like skins —just as kids trade baseball cards. Whatever was owned could be used to trade for ownership of something else.

But as civilization moved on, barter became too complicated to move with it. In fact, barter did itself in by encouraging specialization in production: If I produce super tomatoes and you produce great broccoli, then it makes sense for each of us to specialize and then trade our veggies. But specialization makes us less able to satisfy all our needs. If, for example, a sudden craving for bananas strikes, both of us will have to find a banana farmer to gratify our desire. But what if the banana farmer hates broccoli and is allergic to tomatoes? We then have to hunt around for a farmer who not only wants to trade her produce for our broccoli or tomatoes, but grows something that the banana farmer wants. (The remedy for ever more cumbersome barter was the invention of a medium of exchange—money.)

All these difficulties notwithstanding, barter has made a comeback in these presumably nonprimitive times. Whether it's an informal trade of my hand-knit sweater for your plumbing services, or a more formal organization where potential traders advertise their goods or services, bartering can be cheaper than using the money economy. No need to pay for the services of middlemen, and no need to pay taxes.

Barter is also done by businesses and countries. Indeed, barter is very popular with governments of planned economies. Barter allows these nations to trade the stuff they regularly overproduce for stuff they regularly need, and all without having to use the hard currency which they regularly have a shortage of. Thus, Yugoslavia's overproduction of canned ham becomes the means for acquiring airplanes from McDonnell Douglas. (Barter may be making a comeback, but it still creates difficulties—McDonnell Douglas ended up serving some of the canned ham in its own cafeterias.)

Bretton Woods

Shorthand for a conference involving the world's most important industrial nations held in Bretton Woods, New Hampshire, in 1941. International honchos breathe the words Bretton Woods with extreme reverence. And with good reason. The cooperation of forty-five nations to achieve the grand goal of promoting trade and investment was a spectacular achievement.

The conferees created two institutions—the World Bank and the International Monetary Fund—and set up an international payments system. Essentially, the Bretton Woods arrangement revolved around a foreign exchange system that

BRETTON WOODS

was somewhere between fixed and floating rates, described as fixed but adjustable. The fixed part meant that currencies were pegged at a par value; the adjustable part meant that the currencies were allowed to fluctuate around that par value—but if they moved too far from par, their respective governments were supposed to adjust them.

Trouble was, when currencies moved in their favor, governments didn't have much incentive to adjust. And when currencies moved against them, they were afraid to adjust. Instead, governments just waited for a crisis to sort things out. Needless to say, the Bretton Woods arrangement was filled with crisis. And, in the early 1970s, after a particularly severe set of disturbances on the foreign exchange market, Bretton Woods was abandoned in favor of a more flexible system—called "managed floating rates." See FOREIGN EXCHANGE; INTERNATIONAL MONETARY FUND; WORLD BANK.

Budget, Federal Government

Just like any well-run household, the federal government keeps a yearly account of how much money goes out and how much comes in. On the expense side, the government records its purchases of goods—like bridges and filet mignon for White House dinners—along with its purchases of services—like salaries for government bureaucrats. On the revenue side, it records the payments it receives—mostly from taxes.

At the beginning of the fiscal year, in October, the various branches of government are supposed to set forth their spending limits in accordance with how much revenue is expected. While the budget goes through many estimates and revisions, nobody really has a fix on the numbers until the final bills and receipts are totaled at the end of the year.

There is, however one important (and peculiar) characteristic that distinguishes the federal budget from a household budget—the treatment of investment goods. When a citizen makes a long-term investment, like buying a house, the purchase price is not logged on the budget as a current expense:

Mortgage payments are surely a current expense, but not the total bill. Likewise, businesses segregate their capital spending on buildings and machines from their current spending like interest payments on the money borrowed to finance those capital projects.

The federal government, however, treats its purchases of investment goods just as if they were current expenses. Simply put, government spending for bridges and dams is lumped into the budget along with spending for bureaucrats' salaries and filet mignon. Thus, in a period of high capital spending—like a defense buildup—the expenditures for capital products weigh heavily on the federal budget, making the deficit look larger than if it were more conventionally calculated.

Also unlike any well-run household, the government has been spending a lot more than it takes in: hence the debut of what is often pronounced as one word, *budget deficit*. Now, deficits aren't necessarily a bad thing. In fact, many economists encourage the government to turn to red ink whenever the economy slumps. The idea is that if the government steps up its buying of goods and services, then unemployment won't be as severe as it otherwise might be.

The corollary to a budget deficit is, of course, a *budget surplus*. Here, the notion is that during good economic times the government should pull back on its own spending, not only because the economy can steam along by itself, but because extra government spending could be inflationary—too much demand chasing too few goods will send prices up. That's the notion. The fact is that even though the economy has gone through many up-and-down cycles since 1929, the government has run a budget surplus in only eight of those years, most recently in 1969.

This seesaw between budget deficits and surpluses brings us to the revival of an idea that has been out of fashion for several decades, the *balanced budget*. The notion is simplicity itself: The government should not spend more or less than it receives, but exactly what it receives. Supporters of a balanced budget argue that it's the only responsible way for the government to act. Critics reply that if the federal government committed itself to running a balanced budget, then it wouldn't be able to soften the impact of economic slumps. See DEFICIT SPENDING OR FINANCING.

Business Cycle

The technical term for the ups and downs in the economic growth rate. Although the word "cycle" implies some regular, rhythmic movement, business cycles are erratic. They encompass varying periods of time—the ups have ranged anywhere from nine months to eight years, the downs from half a year to six years—and they vary in severity and plenitude. Their only true cyclical aspect is that ups are followed by downs which are, in turn, followed by ups.

Business cycle chat employs some specific terms: The lowest point, which occurs during a recession (or depression), is called a trough; the highest point, which occurs during a boom, is called a peak. The in-between periods are called expansions or contractions.

The economic statistic used to track business cycles is the trend (or historical) growth rate of gross national product, minus inflation. When GNP falls below its trend, economists say that the economy is contracting; when it grows above its trend, the economy is expanding. The long-term trend of GNP, by the way, goes gently upward—a reflection of the fact that the periods of expansion have been longer and stronger than periods of contraction.

Ideally, of course, there would be no downs. Ideally, economists and politicians would be able to manipulate the economy to ensure steady growth without reversals. Realistically, however, the economy is not all that manageable.

Most obviously, it is prey to events beyond the control of economists. These types of events are called, appropriately enough, shocks. Inflationary shocks, for example, can be particularly menacing to economists' dreams of stable prices.

BUSINESS CYCLE

Consider the weather, a traditional wild card: Floods or droughts can translate into a bad harvest which, in turn, means suddenly high food prices. Or consider the severe inflationary shocks in the 1970s when OPEC decided to raise oil prices dramatically.

Almost as obviously, the economy is also prey to events orchestrated by its players. A giant tax increase, for example, might curtail spending severely, causing economic activity to sicken. Or, optimistic firms might produce too much, causing an "inventory slowdown."

The business cycle, then, is likely to remain one of those exasperating facts of economic life, and good times will follow bad, bad times will follow good. . . . See INVENTORY.

Capital

Any physical item used to produce things. Capital covers a broad range: from humble implements like hoes and hammers to huge factories, complicated machinery, and sophisticated equipment.

As most introductory textbooks will tell you, capital is one of the three factors of production; the other two are land and labor. A classic example of this trio describes how a garden plot (land), a farmer (labor), and a hoe (capital) are combined to produce tomatoes. The hoe is important in the production process because it enhances the productivity of land and labor: Sure, the farmer could scratch out a tomato garden without a hoe, but he can produce more tomatoes, in the same amount of time, using a hoe.

The act of producing capital goods is itself a form of investment because it uses resources to make goods that are not consumable, but are used to make other goods (machine tools, for example). Hence the origin of the phrase "seed capital" to describe an economy's investment in future productivity. If an economy consumes its seed capital, it diminishes its chance to grow in the future. Thus, the amount of capital goods—or, the size of the capital stock—in an economy is an important measure of viability.

Like any other investment, the value of capital goods depends on the income they generate in the future. The value of the farmer's hoe, for example, is not its purchase price, but how much income the hoe will earn during its useful life, discounted by the interest rate or the carrying cost of the hoe.

Capital Formation

The net addition to the capital stock in a given period. Capital formation is positive when expenditures on new goods exceed the consumption of old ones.

Both capital expenditure and consumption go on all the time. Businesses, especially growing ones, add new capital when they expand production facilities, update equipment or replace worn-out machinery. Businesses also run down existing capital when they use it for production (depreciation) or junk it entirely. What economists call a positive rate of capital formation—a good sign for the economy—means that capital stock is being added faster than it is depreciating.

Capital Market

The financial market for long-term investment and savings. Just like other markets, the capital market serves to link up buyers and sellers. In this case, sellers are individuals, businesses, and governments wishing to raise funds (capital) and buyers are individuals, businesses, and governments wishing to save money.

The instruments through which this linkage takes place are varied. They include corporate stocks and bonds; residential, commercial, and farm mortgages; federal, state, and local government bonds; and even consumer and business loans. These instruments also vary in the length of time for which the loan is made—from a year to several decades—making the capital market distinct from the money market where instruments are very short-term, sometimes overnight.

A healthy capital market—one with lots of buying and selling of many different instruments—is essential to a healthy economy.

Take, for example, a corporation wanting to build a new factory. First, it would be mighty unusual to have the necessary cash on hand, so the money must be borrowed. Second, the company wants to make the best use of its resources, so it needs flexibility in the way it borrows. Third, such a construction project takes a long time, so the company needs to be sure that the money won't run out before the project is completed. And fourth, lenders want to be assured that their investment is liquid (somebody will buy the company's loan instrument if need be), so they want a market with lots of buyers. In other words, the corporation needs a market in which a large chunk of money can be raised, in a number of ways, for a long-term investment.

Just as corporations need an efficient capital market, so does the economy. Absent a capital market, corporations might not expand production, thus they would not create new jobs and so on and so forth. See CAPITAL.

Cartel

A group of otherwise independent firms that band together in order to control their industry, usually by cutting back production to raise prices.

Their motivation is straightforward: to transform a competitive situation (many producers making decisions individually) into a monopoly (many producers making decisions as if they were one entity). Cartels can operate in several ways, but for a general idea of how they work, consider the (in)famous Organization of Petroleum Exporting Countries (OPEC). The oil industry is relatively easy to organize—or, to use the buzzword, cartelize. While only a handful of countries in the world are endowed with the natural resources to produce oil, almost every country in the world needs oil. In other words, there are few sellers and lots of needy buyers.

Before OPEC, each oil-producing country churned up as much as it could and competed with one another on prices. After OPEC was formed, however, most oil-producing countries agreed to reduce their individual output in order to achieve new, higher prices. When OPEC got going in 1973, the price of oil was about $3 a barrel. But with OPEC setting production quotas for each of its members, the price rose to over $30 a barrel within a decade. Not bad.

But OPEC has been subject to one of the classic problems encountered by cartels—being killed by its own success. High prices create a strong incentive for members to cheat on the cartel by producing more than the agreed amount. The members figure they can increase their own revenues by selling more output at the higher prices. As these sneaky members increase production, however, they bring more output onto the market which, of course, pushes prices back down. And so, when some OPEC members gave in to the temptation to cheat on the cartel, they helped cause steep price declines. See MONOPOLY.

Ceteris Paribus

A handy Latin phrase meaning "all other things being equal." Economists find ceteris paribus indispensable for pronouncing certain laws of economic behavior. (To sit through a semester of introductory economics is to hear that little phrase repeated endlessly.)

Take the law of the downward-sloping curve, for example. If the price of a good falls, then more of the good will be bought—ceteris paribus. That is, if tastes, income, and prices of other goods are held constant. However, if there is no ceteris paribus, and taste, income, or prices of other goods are free to change, then the tidy law of downward sloping demand becomes very messy to explain. Say the price of quiche goes down but, at the same time, quiche ceases to be a fashionable dish. Then less quiche, not more, will be bought. (You can see why the utterance of "ceteris paribus" is so handy and so frequent.)

Chicago School

Informal designation for economists who are either thoroughgoing believers in the virtues of the free market and/or monetarism. Membership is not confined to an actual presence at the University of Chicago (Milton Friedman and George Stigler do teach at Chicago while Karl Brunner, Allan Meltzer, and Beryl Sprinkel do not.) The derivative term "Chicago Boys" is usually employed by nonbelievers. See MONETARISM.

Classical Economics

A school of thought that emphasizes free markets, competition, private initiative, and small government. The roll of classical economists includes some very big names, beginning with Adam Smith and followed by Jeremy Bentham, David Ricardo, Thomas Malthus, John Stuart Mill, Jean Baptiste Say, and Alfred Marshall. Classical economics dominated thinking for almost two centuries until it was eclipsed by John Maynard Keynes in the 1930s. See SMITH, ADAM.

Comparative Advantage

A standard notion in international trade talk meaning that every country, no matter how lowly, can produce something for less *relative* cost than any other country. It explains why a superior country—say, one that can produce almost everything—specializes in exporting only a few things.

The principle of comparative advantage was first enunciated by the British economist David Ricardo (1772–1823). Ricardo's example, involving Portugal and England, wine and cloth, still lives as the standard textbook explanation. Briefly, the Ricardo illustration assumes that both countries make both products. Portugal, however, is able to produce wine and textiles cheaper than England. It takes Portugal 80 labor hours to make one unit of wine, England 120 hours; and it takes Portugal 90 labor hours to make one unit of cloth, England 100 hours. Using trade lingo, Portugal is said to have an absolute advantage in making wine and cloth.

At first blush, then, it looks as though Portugal is better off making its own wine and cloth. However, now consider that one unit of Portuguese wine can only "buy" eight-ninths of a unit of Portuguese cloth (80/90 hours) while one unit of Portuguese wine can "buy" one and one-fifth units of English textiles (100/80). Similarly, one unit of Portuguese cloth can buy one and one-eighth units of Portuguese wine, but only one and one-ninth units of English cloth. Obviously, the best deal for Portugal is to trade its wine for English cloth—that's the arrangement that nets Portugal the most units. Again, in trade lingo, Portugal is said to have a comparative advantage in wine.

But the example doesn't end quite yet. Here's the point: Since Portuguese wine buys relatively more English textiles than anything else, it makes sense for Portugal to specialize in making wine and exporting it to England. Thus—if your eyes are still tracking—comparative advantage leads countries to specialize in their lowest relative cost products and trade among each other.

Competition

A favorite word for economists, and one which has a very specific definition. When used by itself, competition refers to a pure situation—more formally called "perfect competition." Here, there are four conditions necessary to produce a perfectly competitive market structure:

1. A marketplace made up of many buyers and sellers, each buying or selling just a tiny fraction of the particular product being bought and sold.

2. A product that is homogeneous: that is, the product sold by any one firm is indistinguishable from the products sold by other firms.

3. An economic situation that permits would-be sellers to set up shop, and current sellers to close up shop, with relative ease.

4. Good information and communication so that all buyers and sellers are informed about prices and sources of supply.

Consider, for example, the soybean industry, which is very close to being perfectly competitive. Millions of farmers produce and sell soy to millions of buyers, the soy is pretty much the same no matter who grows it, farmers can grow soy one year and wheat the next, and information on prices is easily attainable.

Taken together, all these conditions create a situation in

which nobody has control over prices. Both sellers and buyers must do business at whatever price is determined by the market, the price that results when all the farmers and all the consumers get together. A farmer cannot charge more for her soybeans than her neighbor does and still find willing buyers, and a buyer cannot offer less than other buyers do and still find willing sellers.

Competition, as outlined above, is hardly a situation jam-packed with excitement and intrigue. No clever advertising campaigns for Brand X soy, no corporate battles between Farmers A and B. Indeed, one might wonder how the notion of competition came to be so firmly associated with capitalism, with firms slugging it out and rewards going to the toughest or brightest.

Well, the answer is that perfect competition is hardly the way of the real world. Capitalism is more correctly associated with the terms "imperfect competition" or "monopolistic competition," terms that describe market structures that do not meet those four, somewhat ideal, conditions.

Typically, for example, sellers can distinguish their products by using packaging and advertising to convince buyers that Brand X beer is not only different from Brand Y, but better—higher quality, snappier taste, or preferred by glamorous people. Sellers who are able to differentiate their products can, in turn, exercise some control over prices. Beer drinkers might be willing to pay more for a brew consumed by hunky he-men. See MONOPOLY.

Conglomerate

A huge corporation consisting of many different types of businesses. It's not unusual, for instance, to have a conglomerate that bakes bread, runs hotels, flies airplanes, oversees a telecommunications business, and sells insurance. Conglomerates don't spring full-blown into the pages of the *Forbes* 500s, however. They are the result of a series of mergers or takeovers, usually undertaken by firms wishing to diversify their risk: If profits slip in one market, the conglomerate can still count on profits from businesses operating in other markets.

Conspicuous Consumption
The idea that people purchase things primarily to impress their neighbors.

Conspicuous consumption was first enunciated by Thorstein Veblen in *The Theory of the Leisure Class* (1899). Veblen saw evidence of conspicuous consumption everywhere, by rich and poor alike. Indeed, he even classified women, who could be decorated with jewels and furs to demonstrate a man's success, as conspicuous consumption. Conspicuous consumption has become an important assumption in assessments of consumer psychology: Advertisers use it shamelessly and successfully to promote their products.

Consumer Goods
Any manufactured item used by individuals as opposed to businesses.

Consumer goods come in two categories. Nondurable goods means stuff that doesn't last over three years, like shoes, cheeseburgers, and cigars. Durable goods means stuff that should last longer, like cars and toaster ovens. People usually spend three to four times more money on nondurables than durables.

Consumer Price Index
Monthly measure that tracks changes in the price level, also known as the CPI. (This is usually what people refer to when they talk about the cost of living going up—or, rarely, down.) The CPI was hardly a big deal when it began in 1917. Very

little depended on it, so very few people paid any attention to it. Now, however, the CPI is one of the most intensely watched government measures—especially during periods of inflation. And with good reason. A lot depends on its every wiggle: it determines the size of payments under all sorts of contracts, from labor and royalty agreements to Social Security checks. A small bounce can trigger the payout of billions of extra bucks.

Just as its importance has brought notoriety, it has also brought complaints about its usefulness. Green-eyeshade critics, for example, complain that the CPI does not accurately measure the real world. Their criticism is aimed at the way the CPI is constructed:

The CPI records changes in the cost of living by measuring the prices of typical items bought by typical families, colorfully called the typical "market basket." The market basket is divided into categories like food and drink, housing, clothing, transportation, medical care, entertainment, gasoline, and so forth. These items are also supposed to appear in the market basket in the same proportion that they appear in the family budget: say, 40 percent for housing, 5 percent for medical care, and .001 percent for peanut butter. Thus, even if the price of peanut butter rockets up, if the price of housing droops a bit, the CPI will record only a slight rise in the cost of living.

All goes well if people's market baskets stay the same, year after year. But here's the problem: People are forever altering the contents of their baskets.

Consider what happens when prices change. If peanut butter becomes wildly expensive, consumers will stop buying it and purchase, instead, apple butter. But if peanut butter is in the market basket and apple butter is excluded, peanut butter prices will move the CPI upward even though people's actual cost of living remains the same. So, too, tastes change for reasons other than prices. If consumers become terrifically health-conscious, the percentage of family budgets going for medical care will increase. But, again, the CPI will understate changes in the cost of living because it continues to weight medical care at a fixed 5 percent. Thus, critics say, the CPI, with its unchanging market basket, misrepresents actual changes in the cost of living.

Consumer Sovereignty
The power of consumers in a free market system to determine what gets produced.

This notion, like most theoretical constructions, sounds irresistible. Consumers use their dollars to vote on goods and services, thus dictating their demands to producers. If consumers like something, for example, they will vote lots of dollars for it. The big-dollar vote gives the makers of that product lots of dollar profits. The big-dollar profits, in turn, lure other producers into the business. There are, of course, some nontheoretical objections to consumer sovereignty: The most damning is that producers can organize themselves into monopolies and dictate to consumers.

CONSUMER SOVEREIGNTY

Consumption or Consumption Spending

The total money spent on goods and services.

People have two choices when it comes to deciding what to do with their money: They can spend it or save it. While decisions on what they spend it on depend on individual tastes—one person's diamond tiara is another person's vacation in France—decisions on the amount spent (and, thus, on the amount saved) depend on two identifiable and generalizable variables.

The more important of these variables is income. John Maynard Keynes first formalized the relationship between consumption and income into something called the con-

CONSUMPTION SPENDING

sumption function. This relationship simply says that as disposable income rises, expenditures will, too, though by less than the increase in income because some money will be saved. Consumption is also a function of wealth—the richer people are, the more they will spend.

Beyond these two relationships, there are several theories about what determines spending over the long term. The life-cycle hypothesis says that spending is uneven. At the beginning and end of the life cycle, when people are starting out or retired, income is low; thus people spend more than they save. In the middle of the life cycle, however, when income is higher, people save more than they spend.

A second theory, called the permanent income hypothesis, says that people save and spend a constant percentage of income, no matter where they are in the life cycle. In other words, a bout of unemployment will not cut spending dramatically.

And a third theory maintains that consumption spending is based on perceptions of relative income. That is, those with incomes below the national average spend more, proportionately, than those with incomes above the average.

Whatever determines individual trade-offs between consumption and savings, consumption spending in aggregate is an important determinate of economic growth. Indeed, it constitutes almost two-thirds of GNP. Thus, as a general rule, when consumption spending is strong, so is the economy.

But general rules cry out to be broken, and this one is no exception. If the flip side of strong spending means weak saving—people are spending at the expense of saving—then the economy will eventually falter. It's impossible to maintain growth if the economy isn't making the necessary investment in the capital stock that underwrites growth. Also, too much spending can be inflationary if the desire to spend bumps up against the limits of the economy to produce.

Consumption spending, then, is like eating. It is strictly required—and, goodness knows, it's fun—but too much of it will lead to unhappy results.

Cost-Benefit Analysis

A technique used to determine whether the benefits to society of undertaking a public project outweigh the costs.

Say the government is considering the construction of a new airport. Cost-benefit analysis totes up the costs of the land, the necessary construction, the noise pollution from air traffic, even the loss of the scenic beauty, and so forth. Those costs are then compared to the benefits from things like decreased traveling time and less congestion at existing airports.

Critics of cost-benefit analysis complain that some of the categories are too nebulous—for example, it's hard to attach a dollar value to noise pollution. Too, they argue that cost-benefit calculations are a waste of time because government decisions are political, not strictly economic. Supporters reply that cost-benefit analysis is an important way for decision makers to get an idea of a project's worth, and that some information is better than none.

Cost-Push Inflation

A general rise in the price level coming from the cost, or supply side. See INFLATION.

Council of Economic Advisers

Established in 1946 to advise the president on economic matters and inform Congress on the health of the nation. Its chief public function is to make forecasts of the country's economic growth—forecasts that usually undergo major revisions by their midyear "updates."

The council is usually made up of three economists, one of whom is the chief, and a staff of other economists. It reached its peak of prestige and power during the sixties when its advice on managing the economy was not only listened to, but occasionally followed. Back then, the ambition of academic economists who wished to be movers and shakers of public policy was to be "on the council." The failures of economic policy in the seventies, however, seem to have soured the whole enterprise, and the brightest economists now prefer to stay at home.

Credit
The mechanism that allows goods or services to be sold on the promise of future payment.

It's hardly hyperbole to say that credit lets the world go round. Business uses credit to finance everyday matters (like inventories) and occasional undertakings (like plant expansions). And consumers use credit to finance spur-of-the-moment purchases (baubles), and well-thought-out ones (cars and houses).

"Buying on credit" can have a sort of immoral ring—is it right for people to obtain goods or services without paying for them? Well, credit is really a kind of substitute money. So, the quick response to any moral objection is that buying on credit is essentially the same as buying for cash, especially since real coin follows the credit transaction. (In fact, in the vast majority of credit transactions, the piper is eventually paid.) Beyond moral considerations, the fact is that a credit economy functions with greater smoothness and at a higher level than a strict cash economy.

First, credit is more convenient than money for big purchases. Without credit, businesses would have to employ fleets of armored cars to ferry their cash around, to and from suppliers and to and from bankers. Ditto for consumers: Without credit, shopping sprees would be incredibly burdensome to mount. To put it in economists' lingo, credit allows people to economize on their use of money.

Second, credit facilitates a multitude of activities by allowing people to have the use of things before they actually own them. Installment credit, for example, lets a homemaker pay for the service provided by a washer-dryer—and process tons of laundry—before he owns the appliance outright. It's just like making mortgage payments on a house: The mortgagee can live in the house while paying for it and, after enough payments have been made, she can then take possession of it. In other words, people don't have to postpone the benefits from a pricey item just because they can't pay the entire cost up front.

Credit Crunch

A situation in which people want more credit than the economy can easily make available.

Credit crunches usually happen after the economy has been growing at a rapid clip—that is, after a period during

CREDIT CRUNCH

which business has borrowed a lot of money to expand operations and consumers have taken on a lot of debt to finance purchases. This strong demand for credit draws down the pool of credit (the savings made available to spenders), leaving would-be spenders to battle over the remaining funds. The crunch itself comes when the battle drives up interest rates (the price of credit). This type of credit crunch is considered a normal stage in the business cycle.

Credit crunches can also be manufactured by the Federal Reserve Bank. For example, the Fed can suddenly and severely restrict the supply of money in the economy, which then drives up interest rates. Typically, the Fed engineers a credit crunch to cool off an overheated economy—a situation that it fears will either lead to, or has already caused, high inflation.

In either case, when the credit crunch drives interest rates high enough, businesses and consumers cut back on their spending, thus sending the economy into the contractionary stage of the business cycle. See BUSINESS CYCLE; FEDERAL RESERVE SYSTEM.

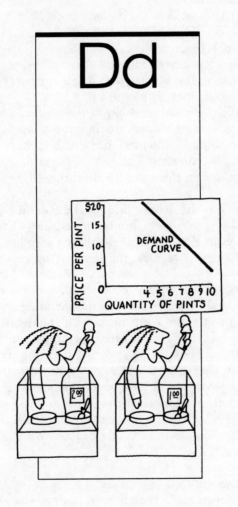

Dd

DEMAND CURVE

PRICE PER PINT

$20
15
10
5

4 5 6 7 8 9 10
QUANTITY OF PINTS

Debt Limit

A legislated ceiling on the amount of outstanding debt that a government can incur.

The purpose of debt limitations is to hold government spending within reasonable bounds of its current revenues. The stricture is based both on historical experience and common sense: government incentives are all on the spending side and not on the taxing side; if left unchecked, government debt would merrily mount up.

Debt limitations have real bite at the state and local levels. Most state governments operate under debt limits mandated by their constitutions and most municipalities have debt limits set by state governments. The federal government also has a debt ceiling, but in this case, the limit is, well, flexible in the extreme.

Congress sets the debt ceiling for the federal government. So when the government bumps up against that ceiling—which it does in almost every year there's a budget deficit—it must ask Congress to raise the limit. What follows is pure circus.

Congress, of course, is directly responsible for the budget deficit. (After all, Congress directs the spending and legislates the taxing.) But when confronted with the debts it has created, Congress turns coy. It often threatens not to raise the limit. Congresspeople make speeches decrying irresponsible deficits. The government bureaucracy, in turn, threatens to shut down operations, to send government workers home, to stop issuing checks for social programs and so forth. In the end, Congress legislates a higher debt limit and the government continues to disburse funds. See BUDGET.

Deficit Spending or Financing

When the government spends more money than it takes in, the difference is covered—or financed—by government borrowing.

Deficit spending, which is a deliberate policy, has three excuses.

One, deficit spending is undertaken when the government desires to stimulate the economy. Here, the government acts when the business cycle hits its drag phase: Deficit spending provides oomph to the economy by injecting purchasing power that is not forthcoming from the private sector. Government spending is supposed to rev up the economy, pushing it into the expansion phase of the cycle. (In this sense, deficit financing should only occur during the down part of the business cycle: During the expansion phase, the government should run a budget surplus to avoid overheating the economy.)

Two, deficit spending is necessary during war. Here the government spends whatever it thinks it must in order to buy military victory.

Three, deficit spending is a way of life. Here, government spending has proved seductive for Congresspeople who spend whatever they think it'll take to buy political victory. See BUDGET; BUSINESS CYCLE.

Deflation
A situation of generally falling prices.

Deflation, like all big economic events, can be caused by many things. Usually, however, it's the result of high interest rates that have forced business and consumers to cut back on their spending.

As an idea, deflation doesn't sound like a bad thing, especially if it follows a period of inflation. Indeed, the very event of falling prices should call forth its own solution: Falling— or lower—prices will encourage people to start spending again. The problem is that this only holds true in theory. In reality, deflation can be quite a bad thing because, perversely, it discourages spending.

First, all prices do not fall during a period of deflation:

Some prices are maintained by the government (farm prices), and some are set by long-term agreements (labor contracts). When high interest rates cause a drop in spending, some businesses will be left with too much output, or more stuff than the market will buy. Now, if firms simply lowered their prices, people would start buying again and the process would be self-correcting. But many firms cannot lower prices; if, for example, they are constrained by labor contracts, then a price cut means they will not be able to cover their fixed costs.

This situation, known as sticky wages, causes firms to cut back output rather than reduce prices. Of course, if they produce less, they will need fewer workers. So, one result of deflation can be unemployment. And unemployment means less spending as people are laid off.

Second, consider what happens in the sectors of the economy where prices do fall. Owners of these businesses will earn less and, quite probably, spend less. And so, a second result of deflation is even less spending.

Thus, deflation can have a kind of ripple effect: If prices fall, people earn less; if prices can't fall, people will be unemployed. Both will cause spending to drop further and the economy to languish. In the real world, then, deflation can be a very bad thing. That's why government undertakes various fiscal and monetary policies, like deficit spending or increasing the money supply, to stabilize prices.

There is one possible bright note for an economy undergoing a deflationary period. When prices decrease at home, but spending remains strong abroad, foreign demand for domestic output will increase. If foreign spending is strong enough, the economy can get itself going again without government intervention.

(Deflation should be distinguished from something called disinflation. Unlike de-flation, dis-inflation is a good thing; it means that prices are not increasing quite as fast as they were, or that inflation is slowing down.) See DISINFLATION; INFLATION.

Demand

Shorthand expression for the relationship between the desire to buy something and its price. It's hard to underrate the idea of demand in economic analysis: Demand—and its twin, supply—are two of the foundations on which modern economics is built. (Giving rise to the joke that if you teach a parrot to say "supply and demand," you will have created an economist.)

Demand has a very exact, mathematical meaning for economists. Learning that precise meaning involves plowing through several chapters in an introductory textbook, absorbing ideas like indifference curves, marginal utility, and budget constraints, and—at a more sophisticated level—understanding the rules of differential calculus. In the end, though, both the tutored and the untutored will come out the same, commonsense place: People will almost always demand more of a good when its price falls, and they will demand less of it when its price rises.

The relationship between the quantity demanded and its price is best expressed graphically by something called a demand curve. Consider a demand curve showing how many pints of cherry vanilla ice cream an ice-cream maven will demand over a month's time. The possible prices per pint can be aligned along the vertical axis (from $4 to $10). The number of pints along the horizontal axis (from zero to 20). The demand curve consists of plotting how many pints the maven will buy at each price: Say, for example, at $10 a pint, the maven will demand eight pints, at $9 a pint, she will demand nine. When the points showing how many pints will be demanded at each price are connected by a line, that line will slope downward from left to right. That is, there is an inverse relationship between the quantity demanded and the price: As prices fall, quantity increases. The line's downward direction, what economists call its negative slope, is due to the so-called law of demand. (When properly drawn, the line is actually a curve because of the elasticity of demand.)

What's behind the law of demand? Beyond common sense

—that the cheaper something is, the more of it people will buy—economists have identified two (fancier) reasons to explain why the demand curve goes down: the income effect and the substitution effect.

The income effect reflects the fact that as the price of cherry vanilla falls, consumers will gain more purchasing power—they can buy more ice cream per dollar than before. And the effect on their behavior is the same as if their real income had increased: Consumers are richer, so they can afford to—and will—buy more ice cream.

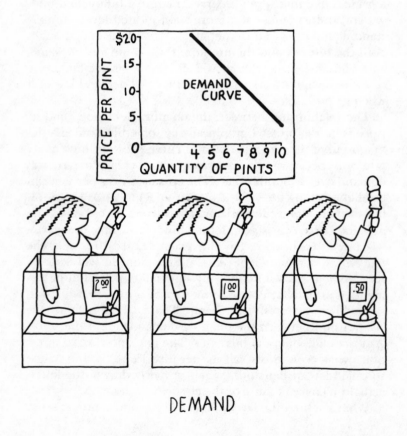

DEMAND

The substitution effect reflects the fact that as the price of ice cream falls, other sweets will become more expensive relative to ice cream. The new cheapness of ice cream gives consumers a strong incentive to buy more ice cream at the expense of fudge cookies. They substitute purchases of the cheaper goods for purchases of the pricier goods.

There is a third reason that demand curves slope downward. As prices fall, people who weren't previously consumers—who were priced out of the market—can suddenly afford to buy. As these new consumers come into the market, the quantities purchased will increase accordingly.

It's possible to take consumer behavior all together (as in reason three) into one giant demand curve. Possible but a little tricky. Obviously, all consumers are not alike: At $10 a pint, some will demand four pints of ice cream, others won't want any; at $15 a pint, some consumers will demand eight, others will be content with two. Nonetheless, it's possible to add together all the individual demand curves for cherry vanilla and get something called the market demand curve.

Although ice-cream makers routinely estimate the market demand for their product at various prices—and set their prices and production accordingly—market demand can be slippery. Several events can upset the relationship between price and quantity demanded.

First, consumers' tastes or preferences could change: In the case of ice cream, people might decide that fudge cookies are more tempting. Second, consumers' income could change: A drop in income might make people feel that ice cream, because it's a luxury good, is dispensable. Third, the population could change: The number of possible consumers at prime ice-cream-eating age might decrease. And fourth, prices for close substitutes could change: A decrease in the price of fudge cookies might cause consumers to buy more fudge cookies.

Any of these changes will cause the quantity of ice cream demanded to fall across the board. That is, at each possible price ($10, $9, $8, $7, and so forth), the market will demand

500,000 fewer pints than previously. And ice-cream makers will suddenly discover that they sell fewer pints at any given price. When the entire relationship between price and quantity changes like this, economists say the demand curve has shifted down.

So far, the analysis of demand had been satisfyingly tidy. There are, however, two loose ends. Demand for some goods or services can increase when prices go up, while demand for other goods or services can decrease when prices fall.

The former category is likely to include already pricey, frill-type items, like Italian perfume, designer fur coats, and racy autos. Here, higher prices call forth more buyers either because high price itself confers "status" on the buyer, or because high price is taken as a sign of higher quality. The latter category is made up of cheaper, nonfrivolous goods, like potatoes. Here, lower prices free consumers' income up to buy other goods, so they buy less of the original good. These exceptions to the law of demand are rare, and economists don't like to admit they exist at all. See ELASTICITY; SUPPLY.

Demand-Pull Inflation
General increase in the price level when demand outruns available supply. See INFLATION.

Depreciation
A fall in the price of a currency relative to other currencies. Under a system of floating exchange rates, the market sets the value of currencies. A nation with a "weak" currency— one that other nations don't want to own—will see its currency decline in value relative to other currencies. The nation with the depreciating currency usually finds itself with a trade surplus because its exports become cheaper and its imports become more expensive. See BALANCE OF PAYMENTS; FOREIGN EXCHANGE.

Depression

When economic growth turns steeply negative for a prolonged period. During the Great Depression of the 1930s, for example, employment, production, prices, wages, interest rates, and profits zoomed down and stayed low.

In business cycle jargon, depressions are just like recessions, only more so. (Recessions are defined as any period when gross national product falls for at least two quarters.) However, the party in power prefers to call any downturn in the business cycle a recession; so depression has become a political term used by the party not in power. See BUSINESS CYCLE; RECESSION.

Deregulation

Umbrella term to describe the dismantling of various laws that regulate economy activity.

Obviously a whole lot of regulating had to go on to reach the point where:

1. Deregulating became the necessary next step.

2. The dismantling process itself was important enough to deserve a special term.

Well, beginning in the 1930s, a whole lot of regulating did go on.

Granted, governments find meddling with the economy irresistible. But the laws and regulations that got their start under the New Deal were pretty ferocious: The Roosevelt administration carved out giant chunks of the economy and brought them under the purview of government agencies. Once the effort began, it—like all bureaucratic endeavors—multiplied. Today, tens of thousands of bureaucrats spend billions of dollars in an effort to direct economic activity. The cost in tax dollars alone is sufficient to draw attention.

But the dissatisfaction with regulation goes deeper—and is more informed—than just tax money. All this activity has not been successful in promoting a healthy economy. In fact, there are tons of evidence that the costs of regulation outweigh the benefits.

Essentially, the laws and regulations that have been undone restricted competition. Airlines, railroads, truckers, telephone companies, banks, and brokerage houses had all been granted little monopolies over their businesses. Thus, these firms had few incentives to perform efficiently and keep their costs down—costs could always be passed on to consumers in the form of higher prices.

This lack of competition created megaproblems. Along with forcing consumers to pay higher prices and limiting their choices in products and services, economic growth was slower and inflation higher because inefficient firms were sheltered from the rigors of the free market. And this isn't just purple prose: Regulation's deadening impact can be gauged by the revitalization that deregulation has brought.

In three of the industries that have been undergoing deregulation—financial services, telecommunications, and transportation—consumers have been treated to falling prices and an expanding array of products and services. Too, the industries themselves are exhibiting signs of vitality: New firms are starting up, of course, some old firms are closing. Although the direct impact on the economy is harder to call, deregulation has already brought diminished inflation and greater productivity.

One last note, the deregulation that has been going on is economic as opposed to social. That is, the government continues to make laws and regulations bearing on safety, health, and the environment. See ANTITRUST; MONOPOLY; REGULATION.

Devaluation

Lowering the value of a nation's currency under fixed exchange rates.

A fixed exchange rate is what happens when governments declare that their currencies will have a fixed value in relation to other currencies or to gold. Devaluation, then, can only come about as a deliberate action on the part of government.

Say, for example, $35 in U.S. currency buys one ounce of gold. Now, if the United States wants to devalue, it will raise the price of gold by declaring that henceforth it will take more dollars to buy one ounce of gold. If, for example, the United States raises the price of gold to $38, then it has lowered the value of the dollar by 7.9 percent. That is, it now takes 7.9 percent more dollars to buy one ounce of gold. If other nations keep the price of gold in their own currencies constant, then the value of the dollar will have fallen relative to them. Simply put, it will take more dollars to buy a French franc or a German deutsche mark.

Devaluation is usually undertaken when a nation is running a troublesome trade deficit with other nations. By decreasing the value of its currency—and thus increasing the value of other currencies—the devaluing nation makes it cheaper for other nations to buy its goods and more expensive for its own citizens to buy foreign goods. If all goes well, the value of exports from the devaluing nation will go up, imports will go down, and the trade deficit will disappear. The United States went off a fixed exchange rate in 1971, allowing the dollar to float up or down as the foreign exchange market dictates. See BALANCE OF PAYMENTS; FOREIGN EXCHANGE; GOLD STANDARD.

Diminishing Returns

A heavy-duty principle of economics. It states that the continued addition of one factor of production—land, labor, or capital—when the other two are held constant will eventually lead to less and less additional production.

This principle is best explained through an example, a simple example. Say you (labor) own a potato patch (land) in which you have planted potato seeds (capital). And let's say that labor is the easiest factor of production to vary.

If you don't spend any time farming your potato garden,

you won't harvest any potatoes. (Zero labor input yields zero output.) If you spend one day in your potato garden, you can expect output to be five bushels. If you ask a friend to help, output climbs to nine. The marginal, or extra, increase in output from the second unit of labor is thus four bushels. A third friend might yield fifteen bushels, for a marginal increase of six bushels. But let's say that when the fourth friend joins in, total output increases to twenty, yet—as you can see —marginal output falls back to four.

In other words, total output increases as you add labor, but eventually the marginal increases in output start to fall. Why? Well, since the other two factors don't change—your garden plot and the seed you have planted stay the same size—you and your friends will start tripping over one another. Everybody becomes less productive.

The law of diminishing marginal returns is very important for firms that have to hire labor or buy land or capital. It helps them figure out how much of the three factors of production to use and how much output will put them at their profit-maximizing point.

Disequilibrium
A market state directly opposite of equilibrium.

The market is said to be in disequilibrium when either of two things happen: Prices are so low that there are too many buyers and not enough sellers, causing shortages; or prices are so high that there are too many sellers and not enough buyers, causing surpluses.

Usually the market will straighten itself out and achieve equilibrium. In the case of shortages, the abundance of buyers will cue suppliers to raise prices; in the case of surpluses, the scarcity of buyers will cue suppliers to lower prices. In other words, disequilibrium is an unstable condition. Market forces will push prices toward stable levels. See EQUILIBRIUM.

Disinflation

A slowing in the rate of inflation. Granted that sounds disingenuous, but it's not. Say prices rise 7 percent a year for several years, putting inflation at 7 percent. But if the price rise suddenly drops to 4 percent a year, then—even though prices are still going in an inflationary direction—the decline in the rate is disinflationary. Don't confuse disinflation with deflation, where prices actually go down. See DEFLATION.

Disposable Income

Take-home pay, or what's left after you pay income and Social Security taxes.

After you take it home, disposable income can be saved (in which case it's called savings) or spent (in which case it's called spending). Obviously, the size of disposable income is important to the receiver. But it's also crucial for the economy—and for the economists whose business it is to forecast the course of the economy.

People spend most of their disposable income, historically about 90 percent. And this spending constitutes a mighty engine for economic growth. In fact, the biggest component of gross national product is "personal consumption expenditures," which account for almost 65 percent of GNP. Thus, when disposable income is growing, it's a sure bet that GNP will grow. Conversely, when disposable income is flat or declining, the economy will suffer. Not only will spending languish, but so will saving—and less savings and investment today means weaker growth down the road.

Dissaving

Loosely, the opposite of saving; more rigorously, when spending exceeds income over a certain period—with the difference financed either by borrowing or by drawing on past savings.

DISSAVING

There are many reasons for dissaving. It can be temporary, due to the purchase of a big-ticket item, a heavy unexpected expense, or a spell of unemployment. Or, it can be rather permanent, due to normal retirement or abnormal profligacy. Whatever the cause, the result is the same: Dissavers run down their assets.

Dumping
A rather inelegant name for the practice of selling products abroad at cheaper prices than they are sold at home.

Dumping can be prompted purely by internal business considerations. Firms might want to get rid of stuff that cannot or will not be absorbed at home—either because the products don't have a ready market or the sale is illegal for health or safety reasons.

Dumping can also be part of government policy. Firms

might be encouraged to dump their goods when their country is running a trade deficit. Here, the government subsidizes companies—pays them to produce and export—in order to restore the balance of trade.

Dumping is outlawed under the General Agreement on Tariffs and Trade, which most major nations have signed. GATT gives offended governments the power to set tariffs against offending dumpers. (Tariffs, which are taxes on imports, thus raise the price of the dumped goods.) This is usually a major event, however, because dumping is difficult to prove.

Despite its name, dumping is not a totally undesirable act. The dumper gets to off-load merchandise, and the dumpee gets to buy the stuff for cheap. The competing firms in the dumpee economy, however, don't quite see things this way. When dumped goods are sold below domestic prices, these firms will lose sales. And, if the dumping continues for any length of time, firms will have to start laying off workers. That's usually when the government starts complaining and threatening to slap a tariff on the imported goods.

Durable Good
Just as it sounds—anything that lasts for a while, usually three years or more.

Durable goods come in two varieties: consumer and producer durables. Consumer durables include things like microwave ovens, gold bracelets, and automobiles. Producer durables refer to machinery and equipment. Durable goods are usually postponable purchases, so this kind of spending is a sensitive indicator of economic conditions.

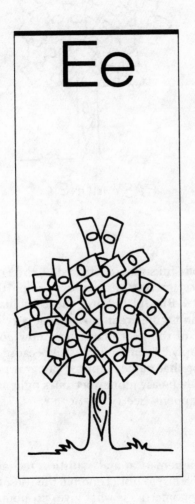

Ee

EASY MONEY

Easy Money
A seemingly blissful situation created by the Federal Reserve Bank to reduce interest rates by expanding the amount of credit available. Blissful because the combination of lower interest rates and more credit means that borrowers who had been shut out of the debt market can now go in to borrow money—"cheaply." Seemingly blissful because the long-term result might be that money lent for dubious projects cannot be paid back when easy money becomes tight again. Which is what always happens. See TIGHT MONEY.

Econometrics
The use of mathematical and statistical techniques to solve economic problems, to test economic theories, and to predict the future. Econometrics is what gives economics its claim to being a "hard" science rather than a soft, social science.

Econometricians follow scientific methods. They formulate a mathematical model of how the real world—or a little bit of the world—works. Then they use data from the real world to quantify the variables in the model and statistical techniques to check whether the quantified relationships are valid or just happenstance. If the model appears to be valid, it can be used to forecast the course of the world—or a little bit of the world.

Consider a simple—very simple—example. Say econometricians wish to test the hypothesis that the amount of consumer spending depends on the size of disposable income. They gather data on past amounts of consumer spending and the size of disposable income. From that, they infer the relationship between spending and income—or, what percent of income was spent over time. If it looks as if the relationship between the two variables is solid—say, that people routinely spend 75 percent of their disposable income—then econometricians claim that their model will forecast the dollar figure for consumer spending once disposable income is known.

Econometrics has all sorts of applications. To cite just two well-known ones: business uses it to forecast the demand for their products; government uses it to determine the impact policies will have on the economy.

There are, however, plenty of objections to econometrics. On a lofty plane, critics argue that the world, or any small part of it, is too complicated to be captured with mathematical precision. Or that, even if relationships in the real world can be quantified, relationships change too fast to be captured by models based on past experience. Less exalted—but no less reasonable—criticisms are based on the fact that many models fail to predict the future. That criticism holds especially true for the giant models of national economies which involve hundreds of equations which have to be solved together.

Nonetheless, the attempt to test theories with real-world data does set economics apart from other social sciences. (And as long as econometrics doesn't claim too much for its methods, knowing what doesn't work is probably just as valuable as knowing what does.) See MODEL.

Economic Efficiency

A condition that is achieved when resources are used without undue waste, cost, and effort.

The concept of efficiency is central to economics. Indeed, it is usually trotted out at the beginning of textbooks as part of the serious, even stern, discussion of how economics is a science that deals with the allocation of scarce resources. The point, of course, is that since resources are finite, they should be employed as wisely as possible.

Often textbooks then go on to draw an equally serious and stern distinction between efficiency and equity. This usually involves a lesson on how an efficient economic system isn't necessarily fair to all participants—an efficient economy might, for example, make some players richer than others. While the distinction might seem unnecessary, it isn't. Many economists use "efficiency" as a kind of stamp of approval. Since economic efficiency is what society is supposed to achieve, calling something efficient has come to mean good and branding something inefficient has become a code word for bad. See ALLOCATION OF RESOURCES.

Economic Growth

This happens when the productive capacity of the economy increases. Growth rates are usually measured by changes in gross national product with inflation subtracted. By this index, then, economic growth occurs when the real value of the goods and services generated by the economy goes up.

Economists are exceedingly fond of talking about economic growth in terms of pies: The more productive the economy, the larger the pie. Now, granted, most of us would choose a big pie over a small one, but crude size misses some important considerations.

Since the point of having a pie is to eat—and enjoy—it, the size of each person's slice becomes relevant. Here the variations are several: If population grows faster than the pie, each person will have a smaller slice to eat. Alternatively, if

ECONOMIC GROWTH

population shrinks while the pie remains constant, everyone gets a larger slice. In other words, a growing pie is not strictly associated with growing well-being. Hence, true aficionados measure economic growth in terms of slice size or as gross national product per capita.

Furthermore, growing pies and/or slices are no guarantee of deliciousness. If the pie is growing because everybody is working harder and enjoying less leisure, then the pie can be said to be less tasty. Or, if the pie and/or slices are growing because people are denying themselves the pleasures of current consumption then, again, growth comes at the expense of enjoyment. Again, a bigger and bigger economic pie doesn't always ensure well-being.

Economic Indicators
A bunch of statistics that are supposed to describe or forecast changes in the business cycle.

Indicators come in three clumps. The leading indicators (like new orders) are supposed to rise before economic upturns and fall before downturns; the coincident indicators (like the unemployment rate) are supposed to rise and fall at the same time the economy does; and the lagging indicators (like consumer debt) are supposed to rise and fall after the economy changes.

Sounds real simple. And if it worked as neatly as it sounds, then forecasting economic activity would be child's play. Needless to say, however, the relationship between the indicators and the economy is not perfect. Although the indicators are right more times than they are wrong, there is no way of knowing for sure when it's safe to believe in them. Smart forecasters, thus, view the indicators with skepticism.

Economics

What economics textbook writers say you'll learn if you read their books, what economics professors say you'll know if you attend their classes, what economists say you'll profit by if you follow their advice.

Alternatively, economics is what noneconomists argue is a meaningless exercise, and what cliché mongers call the dismal science.

That having been said, what is economics? Most generally, it is a roughly scientific study of how the allocation of scarce resources do and do not lead to the satisfaction of human wants. Most specifically, it is what will not confound you if you use this dictionary as a shield.

Economies of Scale

This is what happens when a firm or industry expands its total production but reduces its costs per unit. In other words, as the scale of production gets larger, the enterprise becomes more efficient.

There are several major ways a firm can realize the benefits from economies of scale. First, it can take advantage of something called indivisibilities. Consider a business prop—like a desk—that is not, strictly speaking, divisible. A firm buys and maintains a desk even though there might not be enough paperwork to keep an employee sitting at it all day. But when the business expands, the employee can use the desk from dawn till dusk without extra cost to the firm.

Second, a firm can realize economies of scale through specialization and the division of labor. A one-person carmaker, for instance, has to assemble the entire car. But when the firm expands production and hires more workers, each worker can concentrate on one task, thereby becoming more expert and more productive.

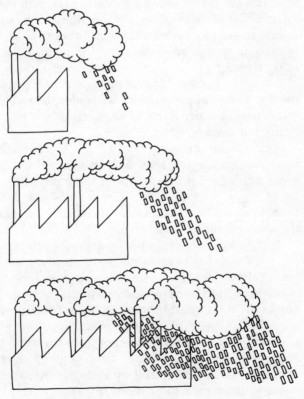

ECONOMIES OF SCALE

Third, a firm can gain from economies of scale by using larger, more efficient machinery. In the carmaking example above, a firm making only a few cars a year might simply hand-paint those cars. But when the firm expands to the point that cars are coming down the assembly line every minute, it can profitably use an automatic paint-spraying machine.

The existence of economies of scale is often taken as a reason why firms should grow bigger. And, sure, there are distinct advantages to bigness. In addition to the benefits outlined above, bigger firms—with lots of physical assets and cash reserves—find it easier to raise outside capital. Also, bigger firms are better suited to fostering research and development which often requires a pricey, long-term commitment. Bigger firms, too, can market their product more efficiently, perhaps by getting price discounts for buying in large volume or by arranging their own distribution networks.

But there are also arguments against the bigger-is-better theory. These, appropriately, fall under the category of diseconomies of scale. Here, bigness results not in greater efficiency but in inefficiency.

A classic diseconomy of scale in large corporations comes from the managerial side. Not only is it difficult to direct big operations, but bureaucracies themselves often shelter a lot of lazy—or downright incompetent—people. Too, it is thought that when workers are alienated from management, they become malcontent.

And, finally, some forms of business are just better smaller. Service firms that need to maintain good contact with their clients are better off on a smaller scale. Smallness might even make sense for some goods producers: a shop producing one-of-a-kind, super-luxe cowboy boots, for example. On balance, then, where does this leave us? With that most useful phrase, "it all depends." For some firms, getting bigger will mean getting better. For other firms, getting bigger will mean getting worse. And for still other firms, the better and the worse will cancel each other out. Every firm has its own optimum size.

Elasticity

A measurement of the responsiveness of one variable to changes in another.

The concept of elasticity is very important in economic analysis, and really not as abstract as the definition sounds. So, before you nod off, consider a specific example, what economists call the price elasticity of demand. This is designed to show how consumers respond to price changes. Now, common sense dictates that if the price of something goes up, consumers will buy less of it. The tough part is knowing whether consumers will cut back their purchases drastically or just a tad. And that is where elasticity comes in.

Elasticity is calculated by dividing the percentage change in the quantity that consumers demand by the percentage change in the price. The resulting number, called the elasticity coefficient, indicates the magnitude of consumer reaction. If the coefficient is less than 1, demand for that good is considered "inelastic," which means that consumers will cut back purchases only a touch in response to a price increase. If the coefficient is more than 1, demand for that good is considered "elastic," which means that consumers will cut purchases way, way back if prices go up.

As a rough rule, goods or services for which demand is inelastic include things that have no close substitutes—like salt—or that constitute a small part of consumer purchases—like paper clips. Goods or services for which demand is elastic include things that have close substitutes—like lamb chops—or that take up a large part of consumers' budgets—like cars. See DEMAND; SUPPLY.

Entrepreneur

In economic theory, the definition is lifeless—to wit, the owner-manager of a firm. In economic lore, however, the definition is larger than life itself—to wit, a risk-taking,

ENTREPRENEUR

clever-thinking, farseeing, establishment-defying head of his or her own enterprise, with the emphasis on enterprise.

Equilibrium

A state where the entire economic system is in balance. This state is largely mythical, but that certainly doesn't prevent economists from talking about it. However, to avoid the charge that they are indulging in magical thinking, economists say the economy "tends" toward equilibrium.

The most important, useful, and nonimaginary equilibrium is something called equilibrium with respect to supply and demand. Here, the formal definition of equilibrium is that state where the quantity demanded by buyers equals the quantity supplied by sellers. When this balance is achieved, the equilibrium price will show no signs of moving up or

EQUILIBRIUM

down. (Equilibrium price is also called the market clearing price.) See DISEQUILIBRIUM; SUPPLY AND DEMAND.

Exchange Rates. See FOREIGN EXCHANGE.

Expectations

Beliefs about the future. While that might sound harmlessly abstract, expectations have a real and important impact on economic decisions. Firms base pricing decisions on expectations about their economic prospects and the direction of costs; consumers base purchasing decisions on expectations about their future earnings and the direction of prices.

But having said that, it is hard to say much more with any certainty. Expectations are crucial but, since they cannot be directly observed, they are pretty much unmeasurable. Economists have tried to slip around the measurement problem by concentrating, instead, on how expectations are formed and why they change.

Export

Anything that's made at home but sold in another country. Exports can be tangible things like computers and corn, or they can be intangible ones like banking and insurance services.

Countries like to export, so governments usually have policies to encourage the activity. But because governments must pay lip service to the idea of free trade, they don't like to pay producers directly to export. Instead, governments do sneaky things, like subsidizing exports by offering producers low interest rate loans. See IMPORT.

Externality

A side effect, or spillover, from an activity that does not naturally have a market price.

Externalities can arise from either the consumption or the production process. For example, if your neighbor turns his front yard into a parking lot, the unsightliness that greets you when you look out your window is called a consumption externality. And if a businesss dumps its industrial waste in a river, the resulting pollution is called a production externality.

(Externalities aren't always bad. If your neighbor creates a formal English garden in his front yard, he gives you a rather pleasing consumption externality. Usually, however, people focus on the bad ones and take the good ones as their due.)

The slippery thing about externalities, at least for economists, is that there is no easy way to fix a price on them. Or enforce it. Just imagine the hassle in making your neighbor-with-the-parking-lot pay for the ruination of your view. (Likewise, your neighbor-with-the-English-garden would have a tough time making you pay for the improvement.)

Thus, the existence of externalities provides a good case for government intervention. The government, in effect, can put a price on externalities, either by taxing the activity that leads to them or by levying a fine on them. The government may also prohibit certain activities outright, like forbidding people from turning their yards into parking lots.

Ff

Factor of Production

A resource that is used to produce goods or services.

Factors of production are, arbitrarily, divided into three categories: land or natural resources, such as minerals, timber, water, and land itself; labor, such as physical and intellectual talents; and capital, such as factories, transportation, and machinery. (Sometimes economists include a fourth factor of production—the entrepreneurial skill that goes into organizing the first three factors.)

Each of these three factors is considered a scarce resource and is compensated for its contribution to production. For land, the compensation comes in the form of rent. For labor, payment comes in the form of wages or salaries. And for capital, income comes in the form of interest. (Entrepreneurial ability is rewarded by profit.)

All of these words are just definitions, of course. What's really interesting about the factors of production—the way they are organized, how they are priced—is the subject of economics. See CAPITAL; LABOR; LAND.

Federal Open Market Committee. See FEDERAL RESERVE SYSTEM.

Federal Reserve System

Refers to both the entire Federal Reserve System and its most visible part, the Federal Reserve Board. The Fed, to use its nickname, is our central bank, the bank of banks; its clients are commercial banks and the government.

The Fed was created in 1913. It consists of twelve banks spread across the country and a board of governors located in Washington. All the interesting action takes place in Washington, where seven governors and the chairperson direct functions that make the Fed a very heavy hitter in determining the course of the economy.

The Fed's most important function is to control the money supply. This is accomplished through two activities: buying and selling government securities and changing reserve requirements. The key to understanding these activities is knowing how the Fed interacts with its member banks. This requires a rather lengthy explanation, but once this relationship is understood, everything else will fall into place.

Banks are required to keep reserves against the money they loan. If you open an account at a bank by depositing $1000, the bank cannot turn around and lend out the entire $1000; it must reserve some fraction of that amount. Banks that are members of the Federal Reserve—which includes all big banks and most small ones—are required to keep a minimum amount of reserves against their deposits. These reserves are usually held as deposits in the Federal Reserve System. It is through its grip on these bank reserves that the Fed is able to keep its hand on the loan activities of banks and, thus, on the economy.

Now back to just how the Fed controls the money supply. The Fed's most powerful activity, the buying and selling of government bonds, is carried on by something called the Federal Open Market Committee (FOMC) that does something called open market operations. Say the Fed thinks that the economy is overheating—business is expanding too fast and/or inflation is rising too steeply—then the Federal Open Market Committee will move to restrict the amount of credit. It will sell government securities.

The buyers of these securities pay the Fed with checks written on their banks. When the Fed presents these checks to the banks, they pay out of their reserves. The banks end up with less reserves and less money available to loan. (The banks have to cut back on the amount of loans they can make or their reserves will fall below the minimum requirement.) And when banks restrict loans (or credit) activity, the economy slows.

The second, but less used, device to control the amount of credit in the economy is the Fed's power to set reserve requirements. In this case, all it has to do is increase the reserves that it requires its member banks to keep on hand. Thus, with a larger fraction of deposits going into reserve accounts, banks have less money to lend out.

A third, and also critical, function of the Fed is to act as the lender of last resort. This activity is accomplished through what's called the Fed's discount window. (The discount window is the fanciful name given to the Fed's own lending activities.) When its member banks are short of cash, they can borrow money from the Fed for a fee, known as the discount rate. When the Fed wants to encourage bank credit activity, it lowers the discount rate, making it cheaper for banks to borrow. When the Fed wants to restrict activity, it raises the discount rate.

Lending as a last resort is required when some event causes financial panic. Say that a big bank gets stuck with a lot of bad loans. Once the word gets out that the bank is having "difficulty," depositors start appearing to demand their money. If enough depositors remove their money, the bank will have to close its doors. (A fanciful way of saying that the bank has run out of ready cash with which to back, or refund, deposits.)

Of course, a bank with closed doors means that no depositor can cash in his or her account, and that people will stop accepting checks drawn on the closed bank. If the panic gets out of hand, depositors at banks that are still sound suddenly start demanding their money. These banks will have to use their reserves and, when their reserves run out, start calling in their loans, or shutting their own doors. In other words, the banking system will be faced with a first-class liquidity crisis.

But the Fed, by making cash available to the banks, can stop the panic. Simply put, when the Fed motors out cash to banks through its discount window, anxious depositors realize that the Fed stands ready to ensure that they can have their cash whenever they want it. Thus, depositors will be less likely to all show up at the same time demanding that money, and banks can go on about their business of taking deposits and making loans.

One of the more controversial functions of the Fed, especially in the past few years, is its role in financing government budget deficits. When the government spends more than it collects in taxes, it covers the difference by borrowing from the public. That is, the Treasury issues debt securities in the form of notes, bills, and bonds. More colorfully put, the Treasury prints some money.

If the Fed decides to go along with the Treasury, it will buy those debt securities, thus injecting money into the financial system. How? By just the opposite process of what happens when the Fed sells government securities as described above. When the Fed pays for its purchases of Treasury securities, it increases the reserves held by its member banks. And with more reserves on hand, the banks suddenly have more money to lend. This whole process is called monetizing the debt.

As this country's central bank, the Fed performs a few other, less dramatic, functions. It keeps an eye on its member banks' lending practices and other day-to-day activities, and handles the country's foreign exchange operations.

Net-net, then, the Fed is an extremely powerful institution. It controls the nation's money supply and, thus, is an important player in determining whether credit is easy or tight, whether prices go up or down, and whether times are good or lousy. For instance, the Fed refused to act as the lender of last resort during the Great Depression and thereby prolonged it; it pumped out too much money in the 1970s, thereby contributing to double-digit inflation; and it clamped down sharply in the early 1980s, thereby causing a nasty recession.

In fact, some economists—and a lot of journalists—call the chairperson of the Fed the second most powerful person in the country. That, of course, is just the kind of oversimplification that gives both economics and journalism a bad name. See BANKS AND BANKING; OPEN MARKET OPERATIONS.

Final Goods and Services
Goods and services that are purchased for final use or consumption. Final goods are distinct from intermediate goods and

services which are inputs into the production process. The distinction is an important one for measuring the economy.

The mother measure for economic growth, the gross national product, is calculated by adding up the value of final goods and services; otherwise, the many intermediate products that go into making a final product would lead to double counting. Consider the production of the simple scoop of ice cream. The dairy farmer sells milk to the ice-cream maker for $1. The maker combines the milk with sugar and flavorings and sells the ice cream to the retailer for $3. The retailer then sells it to the final buyer, the consumer, for $5. GNP ignores the $4 of input and counts the value of the ice cream at $5. Thus, GNP can offer a reasonable estimate of the value of all output in the economy. See GROSS NATIONAL PRODUCT.

Financial Intermediary
An institution that links savers with borrowers. Financial intermediaries include banks, savings and loan associations, finance companies, insurance companies, and pension plans.

The process of financial intermediation is simple. Savers are those who wish to put their own money to work—that is, they want to earn money with their money. Borrowers are those who wish to put other people's money to work. Financial intermediaries stand between these two groups, as middlemen, and pay savers a fee for lending money and charge borrowers a fee for using it. See BANKS AND BANKING.

Fine Tuning
The conceit that the government can delicately intervene in the economy to promote growth and employment.

The idea of fine tuning was put forward by Keynesian economists and politicians during the 1950s and 1960s. The tuning itself was to be achieved through changes in the tax system and/or government spending. (Economy slumping a bit? Then inject a little spending oomph through lower taxes or more government expenditures.)

As it turned out, however, there were several problems in the actual execution. First, there is a lag between the time that something goes wrong and policymakers recognize it, mostly because the collection and interpretation of data on the economy take time. Then, there are further lags until the correct solution is hit upon and agreed to. After that, there are more delays until the solution kicks in, mostly because policy actions take time to filter through the economy. Finally, the economic data themselves can be misleading, so that even if there were no lags, policymakers might mistakenly tune a well-running machine.

At any rate, happy though the thought is, it doesn't work. So, most economists now agree that fine-tuning fiscal policy is an act of hubris. See FISCAL POLICY.

Firm

A business unit that produces goods or services. A firm hires labor, buys other goods and services, and then combines those factors of production to make something that it can sell. Firms hope to earn profits by their activities.

Consider a firm like a pizzeria. To produce pizza, the owner of the firm might rent a place of business, install various equipment like an oven (and a cash register), hire a pizza maker, buy the ingredients for dough, sauce (along with cheese, sausage, and whatever), and then organize all the above to produce pizza. The point, of course, is that the firm can then sell the output—pizza—for more money than it needs to pay for all the inputs.

Ownership of firms can range from a single individual to millions of stockholders. A group of firms in the same business constitutes an industry.

Fiscal Policy

Government policy that has to do with taxation and spending.

On the face of it, the workings of fiscal policy sound a little, well, silly. First, the government takes money away from its citizens by taxing them. Then, the government turns around and spends that money on goods and services for its citizens. (And, of course, it charges a fee—salaries for bureaucrats—to move the money around the circle.)

For conservatives, making fiscal policy gives the government the right to act like a self-serving potentate, snatching a gold ring every time its money merry-go-round sails past. For liberals, making fiscal policy allows the government to play Robin Hood, taking money from the rich and spending it on the poor.

But, for some economists, making fiscal policy gives the government a grander role than just spinning money through the economy. By changing what's called "the mix" of taxes and expenditures, the government tries to achieve full employment and price stability.

If, for instance, policymakers fear that the economy is overheating—people are spending too feverishly and inflation is threatening to ignite—fiscal policy offers them two recourses.

First, the government can increase taxes. Raising taxes reduces the amount of money people have to spend. And when consumption falls off, so should prices. In fact some fiscal policies, like a progressive income tax, are thought to be automatic stabilizers: When economic activity is robust—and people and businesses are earning a lot of money—they automatically pay more in taxes. Second, the government can cut back on its own expenditures which would also dampen the demand for goods and services.

The trick, of course, is for policymakers to find the magic point where the economy slows down just enough to control inflation without creating higher unemployment.

The key to whether government is trying to stimulate or slow the economy is whether the government runs a surplus or a deficit in its budget. (In the above case, the government would be spending less than it takes in—the budget should show a surplus.)

The trouble with this fiscal policy, at least in recent years, is that it doesn't seem to work. Not only does government spending policy have one direction—up—but, despite the fact that the budget has been in seemingly permanent deficit, full employment has not been achieved. So, too, tools like the progressive income tax have not been effective in combating inflation. See FINE TUNING.

Fixed Cost

A more precise term for overhead. Fixed costs do not depend on a firm's output: for example, rent and interest payments on existing debt must be paid even if the firm isn't producing one single widget.

Fixed costs are only fixed in the short term, however. In the long term, of course, all costs are variable. A firm can always move offices or reduce its debt. See VARIABLE COST.

Flat-Rate Income Tax

A single rate of taxation for all taxpayers, regardless of the size of their income, and on all income, regardless of its source.

A flat-rate tax is appealing in several ways, mostly perhaps out of disenchantment with the current system. First, the current system's progressivity, a schedule of steeper and steeper marginal rates, dampens incentives to work harder—or longer. Bluntly put, if the more you earn, the less you keep —why bother? A flat tax, of course, is not progressive—the more you work, the more you earn, and the more you keep.

Second, the current system can be unfair. Rich people pay a larger share of their income in taxes than poor people. That inequity seems harmless, however, compared to the fact that the current system's maze of loopholes allows people with identical incomes to pay different amounts in taxes. The flat tax argues that not only should all people face the same tax rate, but that people with identical incomes should pay identical taxes.

Finally, and perhaps most appealing, a flat-rate tax with no exemptions, preferences, or credits would be a snap to figure. In fact, a true flat-rate income tax would be so simple that the entire form would fit on a postcard. See TAXES.

Foreign Exchange; Foreign Exchange Market; Exchange Rates

The first two terms are a snap to define. Foreign exchange refers to claims to hard cash in the currencies of foreign countries. The foreign exchange market is where foreign exchange is traded; it's an international marketplace whose players, connected by telephones and computers, arrange for the transfer of currencies from one country to another.

But the third term, exchange rates, is not so easy. Quickly defined, an exchange rate is the price at which one currency can be traded for another. But that definition raises two questions: Why are exchange rates necessary, and how are they determined?

Exchange rates wouldn't be necessary if countries did not engage in foreign trade. Trade is an uneven process. Countries have different fiscal and monetary policies, so they have different growth rates, interest rates, and inflationary expectations. Countries also have different cost structures, so that prices of identical goods may vary from country to country. Or countries may make unique products. All these differences mean that some countries have so-called strong currencies—ones in great demand—while others have weak currencies—ones for which demand is slight. Thus, trading partners need a mechanism that converts the value of one currency into the currency of another.

Consider what happens when Americans buy French wine. Americans wish to trade their dollars for wine, but the French wish to trade their wine for francs. So dollars must be exchanged for francs if the trade is to go forward.

The exchange rate indicates how many francs—and thus, how much wine—a dollar will buy. Hence, the exchange rate between dollars and francs gives the American buyer and the French seller the chance to evaluate the trade in terms of their own currencies. If the exchange rate is 9 francs for $1, then $100 will purchase 900 francs worth of wine in France.

And now for the second question: How are exchange rates determined? Here, the answer depends on what kind of exchange rate system countries choose to operate under. There are, basically, three choices: a fixed rate, a floating rate, or a managed rate.

Under a fixed rate system, countries agree to a set ("par") value for their currencies. For example, the exchange rate between German marks and American dollars could be set at 3 marks to $1, or the exchange rate between French francs and American dollars could be set at 9 to 1.

The central banks of each country must then agree to hold reserves of all currencies and to buy and sell from these reserves to offset deviations from par values. If, for example, an excellent vintage of French wine caused a rush of wine buyers in other countries to demand francs, the value of the franc would rise above its par value. In that case, the French central bank must sell francs and buy other currencies in order to restore equilibrium.

Under a floating rate system, on the other hand, the market sets the value of currencies based on supply and demand. Say the demand for dollars is great—either because of high interest rates, good investment possibilities, low inflationary expectations, or fierce desire to buy American goods and services—then the dollar's exchange rate price will be high. A floating rate system means that exchange rates are flexible, free to change from hour to hour, or minute to minute.

Needless to say, a floating rate regime means that central banks cannot intervene in the market to adjust the price of currencies. For example, if a great vintage causes heavy demand for francs, the central bank of France would just watch as the franc appreciated against other currencies.

Under a managed float, the third type of exchange rate regime, countries say they are on a floating rate system but act as if they were under a fixed rate one. That is, central banks allow the market to set the exchange rate—unless they don't agree with the result. The net of a managed float, also called a dirty float, is that currencies appreciate and depreciate only as much as central banks permit.

During the 1950s and 1960s, most major currencies were on a fixed, but adjustable, regime. Currently, most major currencies are on a floating, but managed, system. Neither of those regimes seem to work very well, so the debate over how an international monetary system should be run is still a hot one. And an important one.

There are several arguments against floating exchange rates. Most dramatically, when the foreign exchange price of a currency goes up and down, trading relationships are disturbed and the domestic economy suffers. Say the dollar depreciates against the currencies of our trading partners. While that makes our exports cheap, it also makes foreign imports expensive. Eventually, as demand for foreign imports shrinks, business and jobs in the import sector will be lost.

Too, floating rates can be inflationary. In terms of a depreciating dollar, for instance, the rise in the dollar price of imports both provides a shield for domestic industries to raise their prices and pushes up costs for industries dependent on imported raw materials.

Furthermore, without the discipline fixed rates impose on central banks to keep their currencies at an agreed-upon value, central banks can—and do—pursue inflationary increases in the money supply. (Under a fixed rate system, if banks create too much money, their currency starts to depreciate and they are then bound to start buying their own currency—thereby reducing the supply—in order to restore exchange rate equilibrium.)

There are also, of course, several arguments against fixed exchange rates. To begin with, the requirement that governments keep their currencies stable can create distortions in trade. A country faced with an appreciating currency might not wish to undergo the often painful measures needed to bring its currency back in line. Instead, the government might try to restrict imports by passing protectionist laws.

So, too, central banks can always weasel around the discipline of the fixed rate system. Say a dollar depreciation caused the Fed to go out and buy up dollars abroad; the Fed can then turn around and put those dollars back into domestic circulation by buying bonds. See APPRECIATION; BALANCE OF PAYMENTS; DEPRECIATION; GOLD STANDARD.

Foreign Exchange Market. See FOREIGN EXCHANGE.

Free Trade

A situation in which governments do not interfere with the international exchange of goods.

Free trade is an extremely desirable event. It encourages competition, and thus the efficient allocation of the world's resources and economic growth. Nonetheless, most governments persist in policies that inhibit it. They affirm their commitment to free trade, but fight to retain export subsidies, import quotas, and tariffs. See PROTECTIONISM.

FREE TRADE

Frictional Unemployment

Joblessness that is temporary.

Frictional unemployment is the result of imperfections in the labor market. When people decide to leave jobs, or when their jobs disappear, it takes time to find other employment. And, during that gap, they are counted as unemployed. Frictional unemployment can't be eliminated, but it can be reduced by better information and increased job mobility. See UNEMPLOYMENT.

Friedman, Milton (1912–)

Father of monetarism and Nobel prize–winner. Friedman is a spectacular powerhouse: He has had two successful careers —as an eminent academic economist and as a formidable propagandist.

As a longtime professor of economics at the University of Chicago, Friedman created a theoretical counterpoint to Keynesian economics known as monetarism (or, more informally, as the Chicago School). Friedman and his disciples argue that the amount of money in the economy is the most important determinant of prices, and that major disruptions in the economy come from politicians fooling around with the money supply. Much of the evidence to support this argument comes from his 1963 book, *A Monetary History of the United States 1867–1960,* written with Anna Schwartz.

Friedman's political views flow quite smoothly from his academic work. Since he believes that most economic problems are caused by meddling politicians, especially those sitting on the Federal Reserve Board, his remedy is to have a nonactivist government, to free the markets from laws and regulations designed to direct economic activity. Friedman has argued his views tirelessly in books, magazines, and newspapers, on television, and in person to presidents, congressional committees, and heads of foreign states. See MONETARISM.

Full Employment
When most everybody who wants to work, does.

Note that full employment does not mean that everybody has a job. Total employment is just not possible. There will always be some workers who are temporarily unemployed, either because they are in transit from one job to another or because their work is seasonal. The figure for full employment varies; some economists put it now at 94 percent (a 6 percent unemployment rate).

While full employment is a perpetual goal of governments, it is rarely achieved.

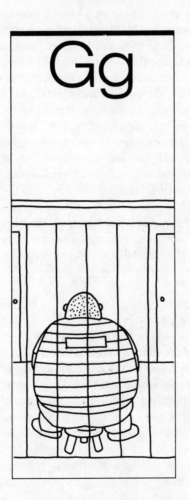

Gg

Galbraith, John Kenneth (1908–)

Economist, liberal politician, novelist, essayist, but mostly gadfly.

Galbraith is unlike most well-known economists in that his chief contribution has nothing to do with scholarly work, but with his popular writings. And unlike most economists, well-known or not, Galbraith is witty, worldly, stylish. Indeed, Galbraith is not an economist in the modern sense: He rails against what he calls conventional economic wisdom with elegant prose, not with statistics and mathematical models.

He argues, for example, in favor of an interventionist government, of the superiority of public goods over private consumption, and he asserts that a "technostructure" (a managerial-professional elite) determines consumer tastes. A lot of these polemics found their way onto the best-seller lists in books like *The Affluent Society* and *American Capitalism.* Many of Galbraith's ideas are not original, and his arguments, or propositions, are not testable. Yet, even his critics would grant that, on the sheer force of his personality, he's an economist to be reckoned with.

Game Theory

Theoretical analysis of the decision-making process taken by two or more players who are in conflict.

Game theory looks at the possible strategies of players who have to make decisions without knowledge of what other players are planning. Each player's strategy, once undertaken, will affect the others. Take, for example, one of the best known parts of game theory—the Prisoners' Dilemma. Here the players are all prisoners, jointly accused of a crime, and held in separate cells. If nobody confesses, they will get medium sentences for lack of evidence. If one prisoner squeals, she will get a light sentence while the others will get hammered. If all confess, they will all get longer sentences than if they had all remained silent, but shorter than if just one had confessed.

GAME THEORY

Obviously, each prisoner has an incentive to squeal, hoping to be the only one to do so and thus getting off with the least punishment. If all the prisoners squealed, however, they would all, so to speak, hang together. Only if all the prisoners act altruistically, by remaining silent, will they all benefit.

Game theory was developed by mathematicians in the 1950s—notably by John von Neumann. Economists started moving in during the 1960s and now game theory is used to explain things like the behavior of oligopolists. See ZERO-SUM GAME.

GATT

General Agreement on Tariffs and Trade. International rules of good behavior on trading matters.

The purpose of GATT is to promote trading among the world's nations. Thus, GATT tries to hold its members to a code that forbids various antitrading practices, like certain types of tariffs and import quotas. These restrictions have been agreed to in periodic negotiations. Since GATT started operating in 1948, the general level of tariffs has, in fact, declined markedly. See PROTECTIONISM; QUOTA; TARIFFS.

General Equilibrium

A state in which all markets in the economy are stable; that is, when supply equals demand everywhere so there is no tendency for prices to jump about.

The analysis of general equilibrium is one of those grand concepts that are useful for understanding how the economy works in aggregate. Say a run of bad weather reduces the corn crop. The immediate result will be felt in the price of corn—less supply means higher prices. Simple. But general equilibrium doesn't stop there. Other prices, in other markets, are affected by the new, higher price for corn. The prices of products made from corn—corn flakes and corn muffins, for example—will rise also. But the price of labor in these markets might drop as higher product prices cause consumers to demand less and thus lead to a slowing of business. Too, the prices of products that are good substitutes for corn, like other grains, might rise as consumers demand less corn but more of the substitute products.

Quickly said, general equilibrium analysis assumes that markets are interrelated. A disturbance in one market will create disturbances in others, and the economy cannot be in equilibrium unless all its markets are.

The idea of general equilibrium was developed by French economist Léon Walras in the late nineteenth century. No doubt the idea is a powerful one; nonetheless, most economies are too complex and dynamic to capture, in practice, their workings in this manner.

GNP. See GROSS NATIONAL PRODUCT.

Gold Standard

A type of fixed exchange rate in which central banks are required to trade a fixed weight of gold for their currencies. In effect, gold becomes a sort of world currency: International debts are settled in gold and, since currencies are convertible into gold, differences among them disappear. But a gold standard does more than function as the world's money —it automatically links changes in a country's money stock with its balance of payments.

Say, for example, that a country exports more than it imports, thus running a surplus in its balance of payments. That surplus means the country is experiencing an inflow of gold, so the central bank can expand the money supply without worrying about having enough gold to cover those paper liabilities.

But consider what happens if the bank prints up a bit too much money: An increase in the money supply will push prices up, and higher prices will make it difficult for the country to keep up its strong exports. As the demand for its exports diminishes, so will its balance of payments' surplus. With less gold to back its currency, the central bank will be forced to cut back on money creation. Prices will fall and equilibrium will be restored. (The reverse is also true, of course. A country with a deficit in its balance of payments will be forced to reduce its currency to correspond to its gold reserves. As prices fall, its exports will become more attractive and it will experience an inflow of gold, thus reducing its balance of payments' deficit.)

A gold standard, then, controls inflation by disciplining the money creation of central banks, and, by creating stable prices through a fixed exchange rate, it encourages international trade.

If a gold standard can deliver such a tidy package, then why doesn't the world go back on one? Well, perhaps the most powerful reason is that many players feel that a country's balance of payments shouldn't control its money supply.

Often a government will wish to run a domestic policy that promotes employment and ignores inflation.

War, which requires a lot of money, is a perfect example of how countries can refuse to follow the discipline of a gold standard: The United States went off the gold standard during the Civil War, and Great Britain abandoned it during the Napoleonic wars and World War I.

The last serious attempt to hold the major trading nations to a gold standard came in 1944 with the system set up at Bretton Woods. Here, the dollar was on a gold standard and exchange rates for other currencies were fixed at a par value with the dollar. Whether the Bretton Woods system worked or not depends on whom you listen to; regardless, it was kiboshed in 1971 when President Richard Nixon put an end to the convertibility of the dollar into gold. See BALANCE OF PAYMENTS; BRETTON WOODS; FOREIGN EXCHANGE.

Gross National Product (GNP)

The mother measure of national economic well-being. The actual statistic is supposed to represent the dollar value of all goods and services produced by the nation's economy. It covers consumer expenditures for goods and services, private investment, and government spending and investment (but not transfer payments like Social Security).

The point of the exercise is to get a fix on whether the economy is expanding or contracting—and at what speed—on a year-to-year basis. GNP is so important, however, that the government issues estimates every three months; indeed, these quarterly looks are preceded by a "flash" or early estimate. So, too, the erratic course of inflation has made it necessary for the government to distinguish between GNP measured at current market value and GNP measured in constant, or deflated, dollars.

As with any umbrella statistic, there are megaproblems in calculating GNP. For one, the government must take care to count only goods and services for final consumption, not intermediate input: for example, the cheese on a cheeseburger should be counted when the cheeseburger is made, not when the cheese is produced. For another, although GNP is supposed to be all-encompassing, it ignores some goods and services: for example, the goods and services generated by unpaid housework, illegal activities, and the underground economy (where transactions go unreported to the taxing authorities) are not tallied.

Hayek, Friedrich August von (1899–)

Winner of the Nobel prize in Economics in 1974 and distinguished member of the Austrian School.

Hayek has taught at half a dozen of the world's outstanding universities, and written more than as many books. Perhaps his most important work—and one that made international best-seller lists—was *The Road to Serfdom* (1944).

In this short but powerful book, Hayek laid out the dangers inherent in central planning and big government at exactly the moment most democracies were taking their first steps down this road. Hayek warned that economic planning cannot replace the free market, arguing that the journey toward a welfare state would lead to loss of both economic prosperity and political freedom. See AUSTRIAN SCHOOL.

Hot Money

Term applied to the large, and lightning-fast, shifts of capital among the world's currencies. (Actually "flighty money" is a more accurate description.)

Owners of hot money—often and unfairly described as speculators—sell a country's currency when they think it will depreciate, either because the country is on the verge of war, faces an economic slowdown, is experiencing an acceleration in the rate of inflation or just plain offers inferior investment returns. They buy a country's currency when they think it will appreciate, either because the country is politically stable (a safe haven), is about to enjoy a burst of economic growth, or offers superior returns, like high interest rates.

For central bankers and other politicians who are often burned by hot-money flows out of their currencies, the term is used disapprovingly. After all, hot money exhibits no national allegiance and its rushing around can increase the volatility of the foreign exchange markets. Nonetheless, there is absolutely nothing wrong with the owners of money seeking

HOT MONEY

high returns or safe havens—even if it makes them seem flighty.

Housing Starts

As it sounds—when ground is broken for new homes. Housing starts, which are estimated monthly by government bureaucrats from the number of building permits issued, are an important indicator of the level of economic activity.

Human Capital

A marketable commodity possessed by people in the form of education, skills, or talent.

Broadly put, human capital enables people to earn a living; specifically, it determines just how good a living they can earn. In fact, earned income can be considered a return on an investment in human capital. In this sense, doctors' fees are the return for their investment in a medical education.

Human capital has some of the same characteristics as physical capital. Indeed, a Ph.D. in economics is rather like a factory. Consider: Both assets require an initial investment—the owner must pay money to acquire them. Both assets involve some lag before the investment contributes to production. Both assets earn income over a period of time. And both, eventually, wear out.

Perhaps the most important shared characteristic between human and physical capital is that increasing a country's level of both kinds of capital is very important for economic growth—both raise productivity. (While one might question the assumption that a person with a Ph.D. in economics is more productive than one with a high-school diploma, few would argue with the notion that a literate person is more productive than an illiterate one.)

Governments routinely provide special incentives for citizens to improve their human capital by offering free schooling, providing student loans, establishing vocational schools, or supporting job training programs.

Of course, people don't undertake to improve their human capital with an eye to raising the general level of competence in a society. Usually they invest in themselves because the payoff in increased income can be a handsome one. (Not all investments in human capital are motivated by the economic reward, however. It's certainly true that the pursuit of more education or new skills can be rewarding in a nonpecuniary way, as well.)

Hume, David (1711–1776)

Scottish philosopher and historian who also made important contributions to economic thought, particularly to international trade theories.

In Hume's time, most major trading nations were on the gold standard. And most tried to keep to mercantilist policies that, among other things, discouraged imports in order to avoid outflows of gold. (Think of importing as a process whereby citizens exchange their gold for foreign goods.)

Hume, however, argued that the balance of payments mechanism automatically worked to prevent permanent trade deficits (hence, gold shortages). His theory was simple: When a country ran a trade deficit, the resulting outflow of gold would reduce its money supply, causing prices to fall. At the same time, the country experiencing an inflow of gold would find its money supply increasing and its prices rising.

Two things would happen as a result. The country with the new, lower prices would start exporting more as other countries rushed to take advantage of bargain prices, and importing less as its citizens found prices abroad too high. Likewise, the country with new, higher prices would see its exports fall and its imports rise.

This situation would quite naturally bring more gold into the exporting country while draining gold from the importing country. In other words, Hume argued that the rise and fall of prices would automatically bring trade flows into balance so that no country would run a trade deficit (or surplus) for long. See GOLD STANDARD.

IMF. See INTERNATIONAL MONETARY FUND.

Import

Anything that's made in another country but bought at home. Imports can be tangible things like autos and bananas, or they can be intangible ones like banking and insurance services.

There are certain things that countries like to import—anything, for example, that cannot be made at home. Generally, however, countries do not like to import things that are made at home, even though imports might be cheaper or better quality, because the imports will displace domestic goods. Thus, countries often try to control the volume of imports by levying tariffs or quotas. See QUOTA; TARIFFS.

Indexation

Method of changing prices for goods and services by linking them to changes in the rate of inflation.

Economies with wickedly high rates of inflation often turn to indexing to protect people when prices for some goods and services increase more rapidly than others. Specifically at risk are people with negotiated wage contracts or holders of long-term bonds, who must watch helplessly as the real value of their salaries (in terms of the amount of goods and service they can buy), or their bonds, is eroded by fast inflation.

In the United States, most labor contracts contain some sort of index clause, typically one which requires employers to raise wages a certain amount for each bump up in the consumer price index. Ditto for Social Security payments—they're indexed too. And, in 1985, the United States began another form of indexation: income taxes. Here the point is to protect taxpayers from the evil interaction between inflation and the progressive tax system—called bracket creep.

Before indexation, when wages rose to keep pace with inflation, taxpayers found that their new, higher wages subjected them to a new, higher tax-rate bracket, even though their wages hadn't gone up in real terms. Indexation now adjusts brackets for the impact of inflation.

While indexation sounds like a commonsense approach to the problems caused by inflation, it has its critics. They argue that indexation will make people insensitive to inflation (no pain, no anxiety) and thus less willing to fight it. And certainly in countries where almost total indexation is the rule, inflation can skyrocket. (But supporters of indexation reply that even in countries without indexation, inflation can get out of control.) See CONSUMER PRICE INDEX; INFLATION.

Inelastic. See ELASTICITY.

Inferior Good

Anything that violates the "law" of demand which states that when the price of something goes down, more of it will be demanded; with an inferior good, when the price goes down, less is demanded.

Although some people might consider the existence of inferior goods an interesting paradox, the explanation is quite straightforward. Take textbook writers' favorite example of an inferior good—potatoes. And assume consumers thought potatoes were less desirable then, say, pasta. If the price of potatoes drops, two things could happen. Consumers might obey the law of demand and buy more potatoes, which have become cheaper relative to pasta. Or consumers, now feeling richer (they can buy more potatoes for each dollar) and preferring pasta, might buy more pasta instead of potatoes. Potatoes, then, are an inferior good in the sense that the richer consumers are, the fewer potatoes they'll buy.

Inflation

Generally, rising prices. Sounds simple enough. But the question of what causes prices to rise has several answers.

Two explanations are known as demand-pull because prices are said to be pulled up by a sudden increase in demand, or spending. Monetarists blame demand-pull on monetary policy. Their argument runs like this: When the Federal Reserve pumps out more money than is needed for transactions, the new money will be used to purchase assets like stocks and bonds, television sets, and cars. Given that the amount of assets in the economy stays constant, this new surge in demand will bid up prices. (More money chasing the same amount of goods causes higher prices.)

A second demand-pull theory, put forward by Keynesians, agrees that a burst of new money will be spent on assets. But they see the primary impact coming from the purchase of bonds: Given that the amount of bonds remains constant, an increase in demand for bonds will bid up their prices which, of course, will lower interest rates. Lower interest rates, in turn, will encourage more business spending and some consumer spending. Again, the surge in demand for goods will pull prices up.

Another group of explanations are known as cost-push because prices are said to be pushed up by a sudden increase in production costs. The wage-push view blames labor unions which negotiate wages higher than can be justified by workers' productivity; companies then have to raise the prices of their products to cover these higher labor costs. The profit-push view argues that companies simply raise their prices to increase their profits. And the commodity-push view says that an increase in commodity prices—due to political decisions by major producers (like OPEC) or bad weather (like a drought in the grain belt)—will spread through the rest of the economy, pushing up prices in general.

Which theory is correct? Probably all of them. That is, there is no single answer. Inflation can be caused by a number of things, some more important than others at any given moment.

The causes of inflation may be muddled, but its consequences are not. Inflation can be bad for some people and good for others. For example, inflation makes losers out of creditors who are paid back in money that is worth less (that is, rising prices mean the money buys less) than when they lent it out.

On the other hand, inflation makes winners out of debtors who can repay their debts in cheaper money. (Some groups are immune from any impact. Wages generally keep up with rates of inflation—most union contracts provide for cost-of-living indexing. And Social Security and federal pensions are indexed, as are most private pensions.)

There is one kind of inflation, however, that is so disruptive to economic arrangements that it makes for losers across the board—hyperinflation. This is a condition of especially rapid and large increases in prices.

The classic example is Germany in 1922–23 when the average rate of inflation was 322 percent per month. Per month! Cash lost its value so rapidly that people became desperate to exchange it for goods. Workers demanded their wages twice a day so they could shop midday because, by the end of the day, prices would be higher. And—or so the joke goes—beer drinkers ordered two mugs at a time because the second beer would go flat slower than its price would rise. See INDEXATION; KEYNES, JOHN MAYNARD; MONETARISM.

Innovation

Said to occur when a new and significant product or technique is introduced.

For economists, innovation is distinct from invention—and more honorable. Invention refers to mere discovery, while innovation refers to the development, promotion, or application of an invention.

INNOVATION

The term itself was popularized by Joseph Schumpeter, who recognized the crucial role innovation plays in economic growth. Imagine where we'd be without innovations like railroads, airplanes, and automation. (Or frozen foods and credit cards, for that matter.) Economists figure that innovation has accounted for half of the increase in our per capita productivity and real wages.

Of course, innovators—those who take the risks involved in applying inventions—are not motivated by grand visions for spurring economic growth. Rather, they are motivated by the profits that accrue to successful innovation.

Interest

The price paid over time by borrowers for the use of lenders' money. Or, more briefly, interest is the cost of borrowing money.

Interest is usually expressed as a rate, or percentage—I will lend you $100 (the principal) if you pay me 10 percent (interest). Unless I am a loan shark, however, I cannot set the interest payment myself. Rates are usually set by the market; that is, rates depend on the supply of loanable funds and the demand for those funds. If, for instance, everybody is spending like mad and saving very little, interest rates will tend to be higher.

Economists distinguish between nominal and real interest rates. Nominal rates refer to the stated rates, like the 10 percent above. Real rates refer to the interest rate after the rate of inflation (or deflation) is taken out. Again, in the example above, if inflation is running at 5 percent, then the real rate of return on the $100 is only 5 percent.

International Monetary Fund

The IMF was established in 1944 as part of the Bretton Woods agreement. It functions as a sort of nanny for the international monetary system, chiefly by offering credit to nations experiencing what's formally called "balance of payment difficulties" and what's informally known as "bust."

Currently, the IMF has over 140 member nations. The fund itself is made up of money paid in by its members, mostly in their own currencies. The specific amount of these dues, known as quotas, depends on the relative size of each country's economy. In return for their contributions, the members get to vote on IMF policy and to borrow money from the fund; the bigger a country's quota, the larger its voting and borrowing power. The United States is the most powerful member.

In 1967, the IMF created something called special drawing rights (optimistically known as paper gold). The value of SDRs, which are issued by the IMF, depends on the value of the five national currencies that stand behind them. SDRs were meant to function as a sort of international currency, but so far their success has been rather limited.

Bankers like the IMF because it can—and will—bail them out when their loans go sour. Economists like the IMF because it issues a lot of good reports on international economic conditions. Liberals like the IMF because it adds an international air to helping needy countries. Conservatives, however, don't like the IMF because it is just one more intrusive bureaucracy. See BRETTON WOODS.

Inventory

The various kinds of goods that businesses keep around to ensure a steady stream of supply to their markets. Inventories include both finished goods and the raw materials needed for the production of finished goods.

It's good sense to keep inventories on hand. (Who doesn't try to maintain inventories of household staples like toothpaste and tomato soup?) But, for business, inventories can be tricky.

For starters, inventories are a form of investment, just like the construction of factories or the purchase of new equipment. And, since investment means a lag between the time that expenditures are made to obtain inventories and the revenue generated by sales, businesses try to keep inventories, thus expenses, low. That is easier said than done, however. While most firms try to maintain enough inventories to cover sales, plus some margin, few firms can accurately forecast sales. No surprise, then, that inventory-to-sales ratios can be variable.

The variability in inventory-sales ratios is more than an annoyance, however. It can have a major impact on economic activity. Say that sales slump and the ratio jumps up; in order to bring it back in line, firms will start cutting back on production. If the cutback is severe, or widespread, economic activity will slow and a recession could result. In fact, inventory reductions have been a major mover in post–World War II recessions.

Put another way, economic forecasters keep a narrowed eye on inventory-sales ratios published monthly by the government. Just as a rise in the ratio can be an early warning sign that a slowdown is starting, a fall can indicate a pickup in economic activity.

Investment
Strictly—and properly—defined, investment refers to any expenditure where benefits accrue in the future.

Investment usually includes the construction of new office buildings, factories, houses, and apartment buildings, new equipment and increases in inventories. The term net investment means gross investment after allowances for depreciation. Economic investment applies to expenditures on capital goods while financial investment refers to expenditures for stocks or bonds.

Invisible Hand
Concept put forward in 1776 by Adam Smith in his *Wealth of Nations*.

The doctrine itself is simple: When each individual is free to pursue his or her own self-interest, the entire society benefits. That is, each is "led by an invisible hand to promote an end which was no part of his intention." What could be more appealing than doing good for others by doing good for yourself?

The "invisible hand" doctrine is more than a rationalization for selfishness, of course. It is a powerful argument in favor of free markets and competition. (And as such, it's quite attractive to economists and rather unattractive to politicians.) See SMITH, ADAM.

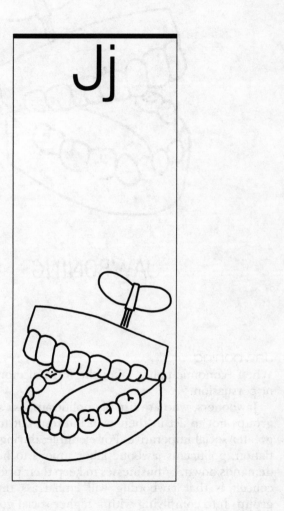

Jj

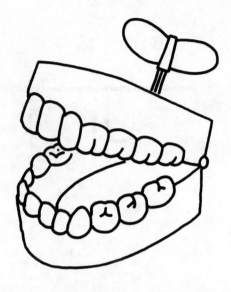

JAWBONING

Jawboning

When economic policy takes the form of moral exhortation or persuasion.

Jawboners, who are usually politicians, ask special interest groups not to act in their own interest, but to respond to a greater social imperative. For example, during periods of inflation, politicians jawbone labor unions to hold their wage demands down, or businesses to keep their prices steady. The conceit is that jawboning will embarrass these "naughty" groups into complying with a higher social good as seen by, of course, politicians. The nice thing about jawboning is that it is informal—no well-intentioned but silly laws are passed; the not-so-nice thing is that it is rarely successful.

Kk

Keynes, John Maynard (1883–1946)

British economist, teacher, editor, government consultant, investor, literary groupie, Keynes was one of those fortunates who are superbly competent in whatever they turn their attention to. But it was as an economist that Keynes was truly awesome.

Keynes was the most influential economist of his generation. And of the following generation. But having noted that, I can't resist quoting Keynes himself on economists whose influence extends beyond their immediate time. He said: "Practical men, who believe themselves to be quite exempt from any intellectual influences, are usually the slaves of some defunct economist. Madmen in authority, who hear voices in the air, are distilling their frenzy from some academic scribbler of a few years back. . . ." In Keynes's case, the ideas he set forth in his *General Theory of Employment, Interest and Money* (1936) influenced the madmen in authority during the sixties and seventies.

Roughly, Keynes's insight was that the market was not self-correcting, at least not in the short run. The Adam Smith notion, which had dominated economic policy before Keynes, held that downturns would eventually become upturns. For example, when businesses found they couldn't sell their products, they would lower prices; as prices fell, demand for goods would pick up and the system would return to equilibrium.

The Keynesian notion, however, was that downturns could become permanent. That is, if people stopped buying, businesses would have to cut back production and lay off workers. Since these unemployed would not have money to spend, the economy might stagnate at low levels of production and employment. So, said Keynes, the government should step into downturns and, through its policies, goose up spending and get the economy moving again. (This notion was transformed slightly by the economists who followed Keynes and are called Keynesians: They argued that the government could fine-tune the economy and avoid downturns altogether.)

Specifically, Keynes proposed to pep up aggregate demand through government spending, even if it meant that government would have to run a budget deficit. With government spending substituting for the desirable level of private spending, businesses would hire more workers to produce more goods. What made Keynes's idea so revolutionary was the emphasis on government action: The government takes responsibility for maintaining employment.

The hooker, however, was the price level. While Keynesian theory assumes that prices remain constant, Keynesian practice proved different. During the late sixties, as the government spent itself silly to keep unemployment down, prices rose. And in the seventies, when government spending really took off, both prices and unemployment went up. Thus, in the eighties, Keynesians are in retreat and other theories about how the economy works—and doesn't work—have become popular. See FINE TUNING; MONETARISM; NEW CLASSICAL ECONOMICS; RATIONAL EXPECTATIONS.

Klein, Lawrence R. (1920–)

Klein won the Nobel prize in Economics in 1980 for his work in building econometric models. In the 1950s, he first constructed a giant econometric model of the United States. In the 1970s—no rest for the weary—he developed LINK, a technique that integrates econometric models of the world's major nations. See ECONOMETRICS.

Kondratieff Cycle

Named after the Russian economist, Nikolai Kondratieff, who argued that capitalist economies experienced long—fifty- to sixty-year—ups and downs. Kondratieff wrote in the 1920s. Joseph Schumpeter later adopted the so-called long-wave explanation which, he argued, was correlated with waves of innovation. Kondratieff cycles are different from Kuznets cycles. See INNOVATION; KUZNETS, SIMON.

Kuznets, Simon (1901–1985)

Winner of the Nobel prize in Economics in 1971, Kuznets pioneered work on economic growth, population growth, and national income statistics: but he will be remembered for his discovery of fifteen- to twenty-five-year swings in economic growth called, appropriately, Kuznets cycles.

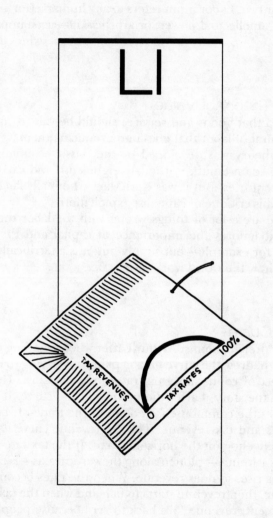

Labor

One of the three factors of production, land and capital being the other two. Labor input refers to any human effort—physical skill, intellectual power, or artistic skill—used in production.

Labor Theory of Value

The idea that goods and services should be valued solely by the amount of labor that goes into producing them.

The theory was developed by the classic economists, including Adam Smith, in the late eighteenth and early nineteenth centuries. But it was Karl Marx who really latched on to it for his critique of capitalist exploitation.

There are a lot of things wrong with the labor theory of value—it ignores the importance of capital and the profit motive, for example—but simply put, it is a terrifically naive view of how the world works. See MARX, KARL.

Laffer Curve

Named after economist Arthur Laffer who, according to popular myth, drew the curve on a napkin while trying to explain the effect of confiscatory tax rates to a journalist. However colorful the story, Laffer did not invent the curve. It simply illustrates the commonsense notion of the trade-off between tax rates and tax revenue. The tax revenue curve itself sits like a hedgehog on the horizontal axis. If the tax rate is zero, then tax revenue—plotted along the vertical axis—is zero. As tax rates rise, so does revenue. When the rates become burdensome, then revenue starts to fall, and when the tax rate is 100 percent, revenue falls back to zero because people have no incentive to earn money. See REAGANOMICS.

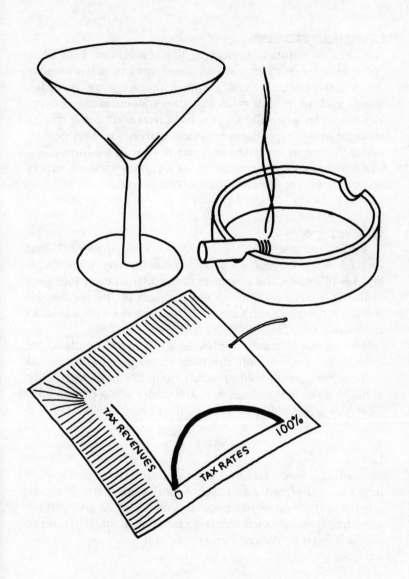

LAFFER CURVE

Lagging Indicators

A group of statistical indicators, like inventories, unit labor costs, or interest rates, used by forecasters to mark possible turns in the business cycle. Lagging indicators are the opposite of leading indicators because they trail economic activity. For example, when the lagging indicators start going up, it's thought to be a sign that economic activity has already peaked and a recession is on the way. As is true of all forecasting tools, some economists swear by the lagging indicators, others ignore them. See LEADING INDICATORS.

Laissez-Faire

A French phrase meaning, roughly, "leave it alone." First uttered by the Physiocrats and then taken up by Adam Smith and his followers, the phrase expressed frustration with government interference with the operation of the market. (If the government doesn't laissez-faire, then the invisible hand can't work.)

The phrase is usually applied to government regulation of economic activities; only the most extreme adherent would deny government's role in maintaining law and order, providing for the national defense, and undertaking certain public works projects, like utilities.

Land

One of the three factors of production, labor and capital being the other two. Land means more than earth. It means any natural resource, like minerals and water. As an input for production, land is different from labor or capital in the sense that it is fixed by nature—and depletable.

Leading Indicators

One of a group of measures of the country's economic health prepared by the Commerce Department. The leading indicators consist of ten measures, including the number of hours worked in certain industries, claims for unemployment, new orders for consumer goods, stock prices, business and consumer borrowing. They are supposed to forecast the direction of the economy.

The leading indicators are published on a monthly basis. If they show smart monthly rises, then watchers feel reassured that strong economic activity lies ahead. If, however, the indicators fall three months in a row, they are supposed to foreshadow a recession. Supposed to. The leading indicators are correct only slightly more often than they are wrong; nonetheless, they are watched by economists, investors, and the press. See LAGGING INDICATORS.

Less-Developed Country

A euphemism for a Third World country, more faddishly called a developing country. That is, any poor country. LDCs are often found in Africa and Asia, rarely in North America or Europe.

Liability

A formal way of designating a debt. Liabilities are the opposite of assets: Assets are owned, liabilities are owed. On a balance sheet, liabilities equal assets—that's why it's called a balance sheet. See ASSET.

Liquidity

The ease or speed with which an asset can be turned into cash.

Liquidity depends on the nature of the market for any particular asset. Some assets, like shares in IBM or General Motors, are very liquid—owners can sell them for cash in a few minutes. Other assets, like homes or airplanes, are illiquid—owners must wait awhile before buyers can be found. The only asset that is completely liquid is, of course, cash. A third-party check drawn on a bank in Algiers might be completely illiquid when the holder appears at a bank window in Des Moines.

A business is said to be liquid when it has enough cash to pay back its creditors. A business that is illiquid runs the risk of not being able to pay its expenses on a timely basis and, in fact, of going bankrupt. Hence, when a business goes bankrupt, and its assets are sold, the process is known as liquidation.

Long Run

Any period of time long enough to allow a firm to change or vary all its factors of production.

Say that Framistan International discovers that its orders outpace its production. And say that it takes Framistan International two years to build new production capacity. Since the only thing Framistan can do—in the short run—is to work the existing production facilities harder by using more labor and raw material, then the long term for Framistan is two years.

For economists, the term long run is very precise: The magic moment of equilibrium is what happens in the long run, and disturbances in equilibrium are, by definition, what happens in the short run. For example, unemployment is a disturbance of the short run and full employment is the equilibrium condition of the long run. (This is what Keynes meant by his famous phrase "In the long-run, we are all dead.")

But the term can also have a very unspecific meaning. If an investor says she is investing for the long run—that she is willing to wait a "long" time for her payoff—she can mean anything from two years to twenty. See SHORT RUN.

Loose Money

One of those colorful phrases that capture perfectly a complicated idea. Loose refers to the monetary policy undertaken by the Federal Reserve, and money refers to the amount of money in the economy.

When the Fed decides to make credit readily available to borrowers, it increases the supply of money. This is supposed to lower interest rates which, in turn, makes borrowing attractive. In other words, loose money means that the Fed has loosened its grip on the growth of the money supply.

The opposite of loose money is tight money. See FEDERAL RESERVE SYSTEM; TIGHT MONEY.

Mm

Macroeconomics

The part of economics that looks at the forest, rather than the trees (as opposed to microeconomics which looks at individual trees).

Macroanalysis deals with big-think categories, or what economists call the aggregates. For example, individual decisions to save or consume are lumped together, christened national savings or national consumption, and are fitted into a macroeconomic framework.

A classic framework—and one which appears with com-

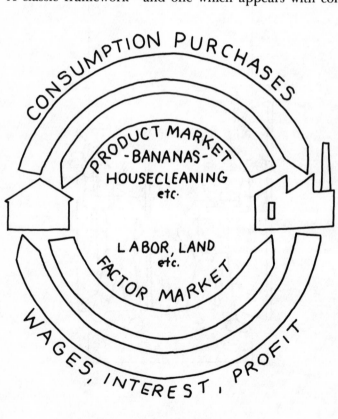

MACROECONOMICS

forting frequency in economics texts—is called the circular flow of income and products. The circular flow takes the form of a giant circle (what else?) with arrows that show the goods and services from households flowing to the factor market and then to firms, and then back again, flowing from firms to the product market and then to households; the income flows go the opposite way between households and firms. The circular flow is just a commonsense way of saying that households offer labor to firms and firms offer products to households, and households pay for products with money that comes from firms that pay households for labor.

Macro also looks at topics like fiscal and monetary policy, the rate of economic growth and unemployment, the balance of payments, and inflation. The point is to discover the relationships among them—for instance, a loose monetary policy causes inflation—and thus get a handle on how the economy, in general, works.

Just because macro deals with big ideas doesn't mean that it's more important than micro, however. An understanding of both these parts of economics is vital. See MICROECONOMICS.

Malthus, Thomas Robert (1766–1834)
A British economist and first-rate gloom-and-doomer.

Malthus is known for his *Essay on the Principle of Population as It Affects the Future Improvement of Society* (1798), which essentially says there can be no future improvement of society because population growth will outstrip the food supply. (Although he did hold out hope in the form of pestilence, vice, famine, and war, which—by raising the death rate—could slow population growth.)

So far, Malthus's predictions have not been realized. He underestimated the capacity for improvement in agricultural productivity and the ability of people to limit family size. Nonetheless, there are still Malthusians who fear that his theory may hold for many Third World countries.

Marginal Analysis

The study of how small changes—increases or decreases—in the total amount of one variable affect one or more related variables. Granted, that sounds dismayingly opaque, but read on; knowing what happens at the margin is crucial to understanding economics.

A good way to grasp marginal analysis is to work through a problem, and the problem most people encounter first in economics' texts is marginal utility. Think of a marginal unit as an extra one, something on the top. If you have a dozen cookies, then the thirteenth cookie would be a marginal unit. And think of utility as units of satisfaction, or "utils," that are received from consuming cookies.

Say you eat a dozen cookies a week and say you receive 24 utils from these cookies. If you receive 22 utils from the first eleven cookies, then the marginal utility from cookie twelve is two. In other words, the marginal unit is obtained by dividing the change in total utility (two) by the change in units consumed (one).

But, now enter the thirteenth cookie. A new, marginal cookie. With thirteen cookies a week, your total utility goes up to 25, but your marginal utility from cookie thirteen drops to 1. Your satisfaction diminishes because, at thirteen cookies, eating another becomes less of a treat.

What other variables will this decline in marginal utility affect? Most likely, when you reach the point of declining marginal utility from eating cookies, you will buy more of something else, like ice cream.

Marginal analysis might seem overly fussy, but it gets its explanatory power from the fact that most economic decisions involve small changes: you do not decide to spend your entire income on cookies, but only a small portion of it. Thus, in the example above, marginal analysis indicates the point at which you will stop spending some of your income on cookies.

Marginal analysis is used for many things in economics. It can be applied to consumers and firms, prices and costs.

Thus, in addition to marginal utility, economists study marginal revenue, marginal cost, marginal propensity to save and to consume. Marginal analysis indicates when consumers reach maximum satisfaction and when firms reach maximum profits. (Another quick example: Firms maximize profits when their marginal costs equal their marginal revenues, that is, when the cost of producing one extra widget equals the revenue that widget brings in.) See UTILITY.

Market

Something that is created when buyers are in contact with sellers, when supply and demand interact to determine prices. (And it doesn't matter if these buyers and sellers are eyeing each other over counters, talking on telephones, or transacting through carrier pigeons; as long as they are doing business, that business is called a market.)

The market is a primo notion in economics. Through the free—or relatively free—interaction of supply and demand, markets play a central role in allocating resources. The mechanism by which this is accomplished is called market forces. While that might sound dramatic, it isn't—at least, not in any theatrical way.

Market forces are the sum of all the decisions, small and big, to buy and sell. Consumers decide to buy toothpaste or cars, business people decide to produce widgets or framistans, workers decide to work for banks or publishers, investors decide to buy stocks or bonds. While prices guide decisions, decisions also guide prices. (Low costs can lure producers into widget making, but if low prices lure a rush of people to buy those widgets, makers might then raise prices.) Thus, economists like to say that market forces set prices. And prices, in turn, cue society on how to use its inputs efficiently by putting values on output.

That is, anyway, how market forces are described in most textbooks. But now for the caveats. Prices are also determined by market structure, that is, by how much competition is present in any particular market. For example, if there are a lot of buyers and only one seller, then the seller has enormous power over the price of the product.

More to the point, if the price does not reflect the value that society places on the product, then the market cannot allocate resources efficiently. These kinds of markets are known as market failures. They include monopolies and oligopolies, and they invite government regulation. The government acts, presumably, with the best of intentions. Nonetheless, when it steps in to set prices or otherwise remedy a market failure, it violates the function of the market set forth at the beginning of this entry.

Marshall, Alfred (1842–1924)

A British economist who started his professional life as a mathematician. Marshall was able to use his mathematical training to strengthen the foundation of the classical school of economics. In fact, Marshall really turned economics into a science.

Marshall was an awesomely important influence. He developed many of the ideas of the neoclassical school. And his textbook, *Principles of Economics,* published in 1890, dominated the teaching of economics for fifty years.

Marx, Karl (1818–1883)

German economist and political propagandist.

Marx and his longtime pal Friedrich Engels zapped the world in 1848 with their *Communist Manifesto.* It begins, ominously, with the words "A spectre is haunting Europe—the spectre of Communism. . . ." It goes on to warn the bourgeoisie that the ultimate product of capitalism is, "above all, its own grave diggers." And it concludes by exhorting the proletariat, who "have nothing to lose but their chains," to unite and overthrow the capitalist system.

Strong stuff. But it was downhill from there. In his *Critique of Political Economy* and *Das Kapital,* Marx laid out what has come to be known as Marxian economics. But unlike the Manifesto, this prose is mind-numbing.

Essentially, Marx takes David Ricardo's labor theory of value as an absolute. That is, the amount of labor used in the production of goods determines their total value—forget any possible contribution from entrepreneurs (capitalists) and machinery. Marx argues that capitalists exploit labor by paying workers less than the value of their product and keeping this surplus for themselves as profit.

Unpleasant as this situation is, things are bound to become more unpleasant. According to Marx, the world is passing through stages on its inevitable way to communism. And class warfare is necessary for the capitalist stage to pass into socialism, and then to communism. Warfare? Inevitable? Capitalists will eventually try to maintain their profits by cutting costs through labor-saving innovations. This, in turn, will create an army of unemployed willing to undercut their working brothers and sisters by accepting lower wages.

In short, falling wages and an ever-worsening lot for the proletariat transform class struggle into class war. The ultimate victory of the proletariat comes when it seizes the means of production, abolishing private property; soon after, the state withers away.

Capitalism, however, has proved more durable than Marx anticipated. Most importantly, the past century has seen real wages, and living standards, rise steadily. The proletariat now has a lot more to lose than their chains—their microwave ovens, vacation cottages, and videocassette recorders, for example.

Further, capitalism itself has exhibited a wily flexibility. The twentieth-century version is really a mixed bag of private and state ownership. Capitalism has definitely passed through a stage. But while what has evolved is different from unfettered laissez-faire and not exactly unbridled government intervention, one thing is for sure—Communism it ain't. See LABOR THEORY OF VALUE.

Mercantilism

A reigning economic policy during the seventeenth and eighteenth centuries that organized trade to promote national wealth and power.

The guts of mercantilism was a system of export and import policies designed to ensure a balance of payments surplus. Simply put, countries tried to export more than they imported. Thus, exports were encouraged with government subsidies and imports were discouraged by high tariffs. Since international trade was settled in gold, successful mercantilist countries were able to keep a lot of gold in their treasuries.

MERCANTILISM

And the more gold a country had, the richer and more powerful it was.

Part of the obsession with gold was just that—an obsession. But part of it was also practical. Gold was a crucial strategic consideration in any decision to fight a war (a popular activity back then). Nations with plenty of gold could go to war because they had the means to pay soldiers, bribe neutral countries, or purchase war goods from abroad.

Perhaps the best example of how complicated and pervasive a successful mercantilist system could be was the arrangement Great Britain had with its colonies, including the American colonies. Through an involved set of laws, called the Navigation Acts, Britain controlled most of the exports and imports going to and from the colonies, and paid subsidies for certain goods grown in the colonies. In this way, Britain gave the colonies the role of producer of raw materials and took for itself the role of manufacturer.

The general mercantilist notion was that the colonies existed to make the mother country (remember, this was centuries ago when terms like mother country were considered quite okay) not only self-sufficient, but able to export its goods.

Obviously, mercantilism meant government-managed trade. And as such, it's not so different from the protectionism people jaw about today. More to the point, neither holds much appeal for economists who think that free trade is the best way to increase national wealth. See FREE TRADE; PROTECTIONISM.

Microeconomics
The part of economics that deals with the trees rather than the forest (as opposed to macroeconomics, which looks at the entire forest).

Micro is often called price theory because it studies how the decisions of individuals—a consumer or a firm—determine prices. That means that microanalysis also studies markets, resource allocation, and income determination. Rather big topics. Moreover, microeconomics reaches beyond those issues to include macro problems. That is, many macro issues rest on a micro base: Inflation, for example, depends on the pricing behavior of consumers and firms and how markets are organized, as well as on monetary policy.

Just because micro deals with the ground floor of economics doesn't mean it's less important then macro. Understanding economics requires understanding both these parts. See MACROECONOMICS.

Minimum Wage

Federal, state, or local law imposing a floor on wages.

This is one of those well-intentioned but utterly flat-footed gestures the government often makes when it interferes with the market. The notion got its start during the New Deal: The government set a minimum wage so the bosses couldn't exploit workers by making them labor for a pittance. It was, and is, targeted at the low end of the labor market—unskilled minorities who are particularly vulnerable.

The intention, of course, was to protect workers by ensuring a living wage. The result, however, is rather perverse. While the minimum wage does indeed protect workers, it only serves those who can find jobs at the artificially high wage. In other words, there may be people willing to work for less, but employers can't hire them legally. In fact, at higher wages, some employers must hire fewer workers. Many people believe that the minimum wage law contributed to unemployment among those who most need jobs—typically, unskilled black teenagers.

Mixed Economy

An economic system that falls somewhere between a totally free market and a government-directed one; that is, an economic system that has characteristics of both capitalism and socialism.

Most economies of the world are mixed, but in wildly different proportions. Some Soviet bloc countries, for example, have a soupçon of capitalism, most often in their agricultural sectors. And some free market countries, like Hong Kong, have a dollop of socialism, mostly in the provision of services. The rest, like the United States, have a more equal portion of both.

Model

A theory that is supposed to capture the workings of the real world.

A model is no more than an idea or description about how certain things affect other things. If, for example, you think that eating chocolate eclairs every night will make you fat, you are using a model describing how chocolate eclairs affect your body.

Models can range from the simple (one equation with two variables) to the awesomely complex (hundreds of equations with thousands of variables—consumption, saving, income, wealth, and so on and so forth—that are used to express macroeconomic relationships).

Economists like to think of themselves as scientists because they use models to test hypotheses. For example, to test the hypothesis that consumption expenditures are a function of income, an economist would first build a model that reflects that relationship, using a mathematical expression of the relevant variables. In this case, consumption expenditures would be on the left side of the equation, income on the right side.

Next, he or she would test the model by attaching numbers (called the data) to those variables. In this case the numbers might be total income and total consumption spending over several years. If the results seem to be related in some nonrandom way (and seem to correspond to what the economists think actually happens—more income means more consumption spending), then the model is thought to be sound.

When economists get hold of a sound model, they can use it to forecast the future. If, for instance, income is likely to go way up next year, then economists will forecast that consumption spending will increase, too.

Economic models are vulnerable to one general criticism: They cannot completely capture all the variables that interact in any real-world situation. Granted, sometimes this criticism takes the know-nothing form of "Models are too abstract, reality cannot be expressed by a bunch of numbers." The more sophisticated would agree that even though the soundest model in the world is a description that, necessarily, must be incomplete, models can nonetheless hone ideas and produce useful insights into how the world works. See ECONOMETRICS.

Modigliani, Franco (1918–)

Modigliani is both a superb economist's economist and one whose ideas have had impact beyond economists' circles.

In 1985, Modigliani won a Nobel prize for two of his contributions to economic theory. The first, known as the Life-Cycle Hypothesis, argues that people's savings behavior is aimed at providing enough money to maintain spending during retirement. In other words, people save to build nest eggs during their working years and then spend—or, stop saving —after retirement.

The second contribution, known as the Modigliani-Miller model, analyzes how a corporation's financial structure—its debt and equity—affects the value of its stock.

While he is decidedly a Keynesian (as opposed to a monetarist or a rational expectationist), Modigliani was one of the first Keynesians to accept the importance of monetary policy. See SAVINGS.

Monetarism

School of thought that holds that changes in the supply of money are the chief determinants of economic activity.

The most famous monetarist—and the one who has pushed its agenda with remarkable ferocity—is Milton Friedman. While the exact doctrine varies from monetarist to monetarist, Friedman's central role has made his brand the classic version.

The monetarist view of the way the world works can be simply put. Too much money in the economy leads to increases in the general price level (inflation) and to economic booms; too little leads to decreases in prices and to busts; and up-and-down changes in the money supply lead to an up-and-down economy. The effect of changes in the money supply is not immediate, however: There's a long, and uncertain, period of time before changes have an impact on the economy.

No surprise, then, that monetarists are utterly fixated on the Federal Reserve: For them, the Fed, as the author of monetary policy, is the most important player in determining the course of the economy.

But their fixation takes the form of severe vexation. Because, according to monetarist theory, the Fed can never be sure when its policies will bite, monetarists don't believe it has any business trying to manage the economy through its actions.

Thus, monetarism argues that the Fed should just aim at supplying the economy with money at a constant rate of growth. Indeed, if the Fed turned into a little robot, supplying new money at around 3 percent a year, monetarists would be well satisfied.

Since monetarists believe that fiscal policy is not very powerful (except for its capacity to make mischief) and that monetary policy should be run like a robot, it follows that they are against most forms of government interference in the economy. In fact, Friedman has translated his free market economic arguments into a political philosophy.

Monetarism is the chief ism ranged against Keynesianism. Where the extreme form of monetarism says that money supply is all important, the extreme form of Keynesianism says that fiscal policy is all important.

The two isms used to be sharply divided, if not downright antagonistic. During the Keynesian heyday in the late 1960s and 1970s, monetarists warned that the excess money creation would result in inflation. They were ignored. They were dismissed as naive. They were, however, right. And nowadays most economists think that *both* fiscal and monetary policy are crucial players. See KEYNES, JOHN MAYNARD; NEW CLASSICAL ECONOMICS.

Money

Any generally acceptable means of payment in exchange for goods and services.

Money replaced barter which, as a system of payments, was extremely awkward. With money, people can directly exchange their labor for money and then exchange their money for steaks or haircuts. That makes money incredibly more efficient than barter, where people might have to exchange their labor for bananas and then find other people who like bananas enough to be willing to trade their steaks for them.

Of course—and this is the point—even bananas can be money if everybody accepts bananas as a medium of exchange. . . . Then people with steaks would be happy to exchange their steaks for bananas, knowing that they could then easily exchange those bananas for haircuts. Individual taste for bananas would not be an issue.

At any rate, money can be anything that people are willing to accept as a medium of exchange—pieces of paper, wampum, or bananas. But money has two other roles: as a unit of account and as a store of value.

A unit of account means that the units in which money is measured—dollars and cents for paper money, and pounds and ounces for banana money—become the price at which all goods and services can be valued. Thus, a steak can be said to be worth $10 or 20 pounds of bananas, a haircut worth $20 or 40 pounds of bananas. Furthermore, by having a unit into which everything can be translated, it becomes possible to combine various goods and services. For example, the prices of all the goods and services in the economy can be added together to produce one measure of economic activity, or gross national product. (Nothing more, really, than the old trick of combining apples and oranges.)

A store of value means that money can be used to warehouse wealth for future purchases. Sellers will accept money today, even if they have no immediate plans to spend it, because they assume it will keep its value over time. Bananas, of course, would make lousy money—they might rot away before they could be spent. Not that paper money is perfect. Inflation could erode the value of paper money just as surely as oxidation erodes the value of bananas. Just not as quickly. (Usually.) See BARTER.

Money Illusion

The psychological response to changes in the nominal value of money—usually wages—rather than to changes in its purchasing power.

The money illusion is used to illustrate the impact of inflation on behavior. Say, the price level goes up 3 percent a year, and say that wages, too, go up 3 percent a year. People suffering from the money illusion think that the increase in wages has increased their purchasing power by 3 percent, when, of course, the rise in inflation has just left it constant.

Thus, if the money illusion holds, workers might continue to work for the same wages during periods of inflation even though inflation is eroding their purchasing power and reducing their *real* wages.

Many economists think that the money illusion is itself an

illusion. They argue that people are well aware of the effects of inflation (and deflation) and respond accordingly, and quickly. See RATIONAL EXPECTATIONS.

Money Supply

All the money existing in an economy. But wickedly difficult to measure.

The narrowest measure of the money supply is called M1: It includes coins and currency in circulation and certain types of checking accounts. Next comes M2, which includes M1 plus certain types of small savings accounts. And then comes M3, which includes all the money in M2 plus the big money accounts held by individuals, corporations, and institutions.

The Federal Reserve tries to keep track of the money supply to control it. That is, the Fed estimates how much money is actually out there in the economy and how much money there should be, and then decides how much to supply. For an explanation of why the Fed should go through all this trouble—and it's more troublesome than this entry indicates —See FEDERAL RESERVE SYSTEM.

Monopoly

A market with only one seller.

If you are a seller, a monopoly is a nice thing to have. You can set a price higher than it would be under competitive conditions and rake in enormous profits. If you are a buyer, however, a monopoly is a nasty thing to face. You will have to pay that high price, and you may even encounter a shortage of product. In other words, high price and low output go together. The monopolist produces just enough to ensure plump profits, and that means less output and higher prices than would prevail in a competitive market.

Since—obviously—all sellers would like to have monopolies, why isn't the market dominated by monopolies? Two reasons. First, it is impossible to maintain a monopoly without what economists call barriers to entry. (If a business person sets up a monopoly in making framistans, the giant profits which accrue will only signal other business people to produce framistans, too. Unless, of course, the others are prevented from setting up shop.)

Barriers to entry can take several forms. If framistan production takes an immense capital outlay, for example, other —less wealthy—firms may face a financial barrier. Or, if making framistans requires specially skilled craftspeople, then other firms might face a lack-of-talent barrier.

Perhaps the most common—and most effective—barrier to entry is through legal restrictions. The firm that first discovered how to make framistans might enjoy a monopoly that comes from having an exclusive patent or copyright, for instance. Usually, however, the government grants monopolies on some notion of serving the public: Countries can give air carriers the right to fly certain routes, states can give power authorities the right to provide electricity, and cities can give a garbage collector the right to cart away garbage.

But what the government allows, it can also prevent. And that is the second reason why the economy isn't chock full of monopolies. When barriers to entry exist, the government— through its antitrust laws—can restrain companies from becoming monopolies.

Many firms, however, enjoy a certain amount of freedom in setting their prices without enjoying an actual monopoly. It is arguable, for example, that beer is all pretty much the same, and thus beer makers face a competitive market. It is arguable, but not exactly true. Beer makers have been able to differentiate their products so that certain brands command such fierce loyalty that makers can charge more without losing all their customers. This kind of market, which falls somewhere between monopoly and competition, is called monopolistic competition. See REGULATION.

Monopsony
A market with one buyer. (As opposed to a monopoly which is a market with one seller.)

Just as a monopolist has the power to set the price for his or her product, a monopsonist can set the price at which he or she will buy. Monopsonies are rarer than monopolies, but they do exist. In a company town where there is only one buyer of labor, for example, the employer has power over the wage level. (If a worker thinks his wage is too low, he has a choice—get on unemployment or get out of town.)

Multinational Corporation
A firm that operates in more than one country, usually through a wholly owned subsidiary.

Multiplier
A shorthand way of capturing a complicated process by which changes in spending affect the level of national income.

To get an idea of how the multiplier works, consider the following example of how a rise in investment spending works its way through the economy to produce a higher gross national product. Say that a firm increases its investment spending by $100 million by building a new factory. And say that this initial increase in spending shows up in wages paid to the factory builders. (It could also show up in higher profits, rents to the owners of the land, or interest payments.)

Some of this $100 million will be spent by the recipients, generating a second-round increase in national income. Say, for example, of the original $100 million, three-quarters of it, or $75 million, is respent. Thus, the initial $100 million has now yielded a $175-million increase in national income.

But it doesn't stop here either. This round of spending will result in more wages for other workers because the recipients of the $75 million will, in turn, respend three-quarters of it—

or $56 million—for a total increase of $231 million in national income.

And so it goes. Each round of spending will generate another round, as one worker's spending puts money in the pockets of another worker. By the time the increases are too small to measure, $400 million will have been added to national income. That is, national income will get a $400-million boost from the original $100 million. A quadruple bang for a buck.

In this case, the actual number attached to the multiplier is four. The size of the multiplier is based on a marginal propensity to consume, or spend, three-quarters of every dollar. Note that the flip side of spending is saving, so that a marginal propensity to consume three-quarters of every dollar means that one-fourth of every dollar is saved. (And the mathematically adept might also note that the multiplier is the reciprocal, or upside-down, of the marginal propensity to save.) This saving "leakage" stops the multiplier from generating income increases forever.

The multiplier is a mainstay in Keynesian fiscal policy. It's used to estimate the impact that increases in government spending or tax cuts will have on national income. Despite this seeming precision, however, multipliers have proved, in practice, to be less than precise. See MARGINAL ANALYSIS.

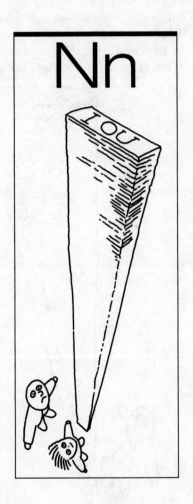

National Debt

The federal government's total outstanding debt. (Note that this is different from the federal budget deficit, which is just the debt incurred by the government over one fiscal year.)

In a world of balanced budgets where government's revenues equaled its expenditures, there would be no national debt; that is, the government would have no need to borrow.

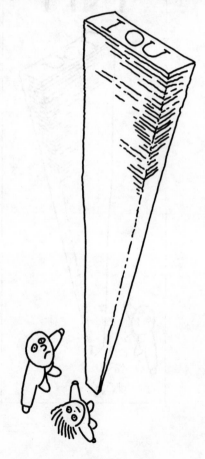

NATIONAL DEBT

In the real world, however, government has been spending more than it takes in, and thus it has been borrowing to cover the difference. The total of these budget deficits amassed over the years is called the national debt, and amassed is the right word for it. The absolute size of the debt is over $2 trillion.

A growing debt means a growing need to get somebody to pay cash money to service the interest on that debt, if not to pay back some of the principal. There are two ways to get this money: The government can print some up, courting a bout of inflation; or it can increase taxes, courting a slowdown in economic activity. Neither route is appealing.

Nonetheless, there is another—less alarming—perspective from which to view the debt. First, the debt is something we owe ourselves. Interest payments on the debt, as long as they are paid to U.S. citizens, are like transfer payments. (Follow this: The government borrows money by exchanging its debt securities—Treasury bonds, for example—for cash money, some of which goes to pay interest on previously issued debt securities.)

Second, sheer size is a little misleading. The national debt has grown, but so has the economy. Indeed, when expressed as a percent of gross national product, the debt actually declined during the 1960s and early 1970s (though it started to rise again during the 1980s). And finally, inflation—which always favors debtors over creditors—has reduced the value of the debt. For example, when the $1.6 trillion of 1984 debt is adjusted for inflation, a full $4 billion disappears.

National Income

National income is another way of saying gross national product. It designates the money flow from the total earnings of all the factors of production. National income includes wages and salaries, interest, rental income, and profits.

Keeping track of national income is the province of the Department of Commerce. In fact, the statistical collection of all sorts of measurements taken of the economy is called the National Income and Products Accounts. Most of the series in NIPA are published monthly.

Nationalization; Nationalized Industry

Nationalization is what happens when government takes over a business or industry that had been owned privately, usually by stockholders. A nationalized industry is what results from nationalization.

Whether nationalization is an act of stupidity or enlightenment is a matter of hot debate. Supporters of nationalization argue that it creates the opportunity to realize economies of scale and/or that it removes the opportunity for a monopoly to gouge the public. (These are economic reasons; occasionally, however, government seizure is an act of pure politics, done to eliminate foreign ownership.)

Critics, on the other hand, argue that nationalization leads to inefficiency because state industries generate large, costly, and wasteful bureaucracies.

State ownership of large sectors of the economy—such as telecommunications, banking, power generation, and railways—are usually the province of socialist and less developed countries. But most countries indulge in some form of nationalization.

Negative Income Tax

An idea that is part of the public policy debate on how to make sure that poor people don't go hungry and homeless without, at the same time, making them permanent welfare recipients.

Roughly, a negative income tax would work like this: The government would determine a poverty line—a point under which family income would not be allowed to slip—and then pay whatever amount brings people to that line. (If a family earned no money, for example, they would get the full transfer payment.) Taxes would be levied on a progressive basis only on income above the poverty line.

The negative income tax, which is actually an income subsidy, has several virtues. First, with a certain minimum income ensured, people would still have incentives to earn money because they would keep some portion of their earnings above the poverty line. And second, it could replace the current unwieldy, inefficient, and expensive welfare system.

While the idea has support from both liberals and conservatives alike, it was the brainchild of conservative economist Milton Friedman.

Neoclassical Economics
A school of thought that, obviously, branched off from classical economics.

Early names here include William Jevons (British), Karl Menger (Austrian), and Léon Walras (French); but perhaps the most famous neoclassical economist was Alfred Marshall (British). While neoclassical thought reflects the classical emphasis on the importance of markets and competition, it expresses those relationships with sophisticated mathematics and statistics.

Net National Product
Gross national product minus depreciation. See DEPRECIATION.

Net Worth
The value of a company after total liabilities are subtracted from total assets. If that number is positive, then the company is said to have a positive net worth. If the number is negative, then the company is said to have a negative net worth—a condition that usually leads to bankruptcy.

New Classical Economics

School of thought that holds that the market produces the best solutions to economic problems.

Granted, that definition sounds just like the definition for classical economics, and granted, the new classical economics (NCE) does take strength from some of the same ideas; nevertheless, there are important differences. New classical economics really is new. It's equipped with the latest mathematical techniques, a bunch of theoretical refinements, and an undeniable sophistication. In fact, NCE has emerged as a major alternative to Keynesian and monetarist thinking.

Most importantly, NCE takes the pivotal assumption in microeconomics—that markets work—and applies it to macroeconomics. On the face of it, this might not seem to be a major achievement. Nonetheless, the chief theoretical embarrassment for Keynesian economists is that the assumptions they believe to be true in micro cannot be translated into their macro framework.

For example, a key tenet in microeconomics is that the market equilibrates supply and demand through prices. (Fancy talk for saying that prices will adjust so that buyers and sellers can make transactions.) Keynesian macro theory, however, says that prices, especially wages, are sticky—they don't adjust. And since some prices don't fall in response to falling demand, government must step in to replace private demand by public spending.

NCE also translates the micro notion of maximization, or rational expectations, into the macro realm. Microeconomics assumes that people maximize by behaving to further their own best interest. By assuming that the same holds in the macro realm, NCE argues that people react to changes in the economy by protecting themselves; that is, people will anticipate government shifts in policies in response to economic changes. Thus, it's difficult for the government to surprise its citizens into behaving against their own best interests. Again, this is different from the old Keynesian macro notion that the government, by manipulating people's behavior through its policies, can manage the economy.

Needless to say, NCE goes on to argue that active government management of the economy is, at best, ineffective; at worst, government management makes things worse. Further, NCE places a great emphasis on the power of monetary policy—particularly its power to cause mischief like inflation.

In terms of policy, then, the bottom line for the new classical economics is that the government should not interfere with markets, that both fiscal and monetary policy should be rather passive and predictable. See KEYNES, JOHN MAYNARD; MONETARISM; RATIONAL EXPECTATIONS.

NIPA. See NATIONAL INCOME.

Nonprice Competition

A way of competing for buyers without lowering prices.

Say that Framistan Perfume wishes to increase its market share without lowering its price. Framistan can do several things. It can "differentiate" its perfume by changing its packaging or quality; it can advertise that its perfume provides the wearer with superior sexual appeal; or it can offer buyers a free tote bag with each purchase. While these strategies might sound a bit hokey, they are usually effective.

Nonprice competition often results in more varieties, or styles, of product being offered to consumers.

Normative Economics

The usual definition of normative economics says something about its being the branch that inquires into "what ought to be...." What goods and services ought to be produced, who ought to own resources, how income ought to be distributed. This is just an upstanding way of saying that economic questions, or policy issues, involve value judgments. In other words, what's called normative economics is what happens when people pronounce on what is good and what is bad.

But value judgments depend on one's perspective. An unemployed, unskilled worker has a different view of how tax policy affects income distribution than does a boss or an heiress. Thus, a more accurate definition of normative economics would be: The phrase applied to the moral side of public policy debates. See POSITIVE ECONOMICS.

Oligopoly

A market that is dominated by a few large firms.

In terms of market structure, an oligopoly falls between monopoly (one producer) and competition (many producers). In terms of the firms' practices, however, an oligopoly can transform itself into either one. If the firms agree to set prices, an oligopoly becomes a monopoly; if the firms enter into a price war, an oligopoly becomes competitive.

The incentive for becoming a monopoly by price-fixing is clear: All the firms can raise their prices and enjoy larger profits. In the competitive case, however, the incentive only operates for the first firm, which, when it cuts its price, can grab a bigger share of the market. (After that, of course, the rest of the firms follow suit and the ensuing price war will reduce everybody's profits.)

Despite these incentives, oligopolies—and their prices— usually remain stable. For two simple reasons: If firms collude on prices, they will be in violation of the antitrust laws; and if they engage in a price war, their profits will suffer. Since either outcome is not terribly desirable, the result is

OLIGOPOLY

that oligopolistic firms will keep their prices close together and compete, instead, in other ways. Particularly by advertising. (Just check out the money that oligopolies—from carmakers to beer brewers—spend on advertising aimed at touting product characteristics other than price tags.)

Oligopolies are not desirable. They can set prices higher than might be allowed under competitive conditions (and generally show higher profits despite the tons of money spent on advertising).

Open Market Operations

Name given to the activity of buying and selling government securities when it's done by the Federal Reserve System.

Open market operations are set into motion at the monthly meeting of the Federal Open Market Committee (FOMC). At these gatherings, the governors of the Federal Reserve in Washington, along with presidents of five regional Federal Reserve Banks, vote on how to conduct monetary policy over the near term. Just what goes on at these meetings is a big secret until, weeks later, the minutes are published.

The operations themselves consist of the Fed buying or selling government securities. If, for example, the FOMC decides that the economy is growing too fast—and inflation threatens—it takes securities from its own portfolio holdings and sells them on the open market.

The buyers pay for the securities by giving the Fed checks drawn on their banks. When the Fed presents those checks for payment, an interesting thing happens. The banks lose some of their "balances with the Fed," which means that their reserves are reduced. When bank reserves (assets) are reduced, the banks must, of course, reduce the amount of their deposits (liabilities). And, since the banking system is a fractional reserve system—where reserves back only a fraction of loanable money—fewer reserves means a whole lot fewer deposits or bank-created money.

In other words, the sale of government securities reduces

the amount of loan money available from banks, which means there is less credit in the system. Less credit, in turn, means higher interest rates. Higher interest rates, in turn, means less business activity. Less business activity, in turn, means slower economic growth.

There is, thus, a rather long chain of events between the FOMC decision that the economy is overheating and the actual slowing of the economy. And in a big, complicated economy, a long chain of events leaves a lot of room for random mess-ups. Simply put, policy is one thing, results another. Nonetheless, open market operations are considered to be the most powerful tool the Fed has in its management of monetary policy. See BANKS AND BANKING; FEDERAL RESERVE SYSTEM.

Opportunity Cost

A measure of what could have been. The amount of money given up when resources are used to produce one thing instead of something else.

Opportunity cost is a classic kind of economist's notion. For an accountant, for example, a cost is a cost; it is whatever must be, or has been, paid. For an economist, however, a cost is mixed up with another notion, one about scarce resources. That is, the real cost of using scarce resources to produce a tractor is the value of other things that cannot be produced when those resources are used to produce the tractor.

By this logic, everything has a cost. Even leisure time—the cost of spending an afternoon playing tennis is what you could earn working.

Opportunity cost is useful in deciding between two alternatives. The usual example given in economics texts is about a self-employed person who could earn, say, $40,000 a year as an advertising executive and chooses instead to open a doughnut shop. If the doughnut maker takes home $20,000, he or she is $20,000 in the hole, when the opportunity cost of his or her alternative labor as an ad exec is considered.

Pareto Optimality

Named after Italian economist Vilfredo Pareto (1848–1923), pareto optimality represents a kind of a magic moment when resources are being used so efficiently that nobody can be made better off without making somebody else worse off.

As a specific notion, pareto optimality has a certain power because resources are usually being used inefficiently. Thus, any remedy will improve the welfare of some without damaging the welfare of others; optimality is something to aim for.

Planned Economy

Many definitions are possible (and accurate) here, but roughly a planned economy is one that eschews the price mechanism as the main way to allocate resources.

Typically, it is government that does the planning; that

PLANNED ECONOMY

is, the government decides on what and how things are produced, where investment money flows, and how income is distributed. Typically, too, government owns large chunks of the economy.

While the goal of a planned economy is worthy—to maximize the social welfare of all members of the society—the economic costs are usually big. Most obviously, government allocation of resources is dramatically imperfect. Granted, such allocation is meant to be inefficient in the sense that government decides on questions of social welfare first and economic ones second; nonetheless, the creation of a bureaucracy to oversee all economic matters often results both in bad decisions and in bad decisions that are permitted to persist.

All nations indulge in some forms of planning, but the most extreme forms are found in communist nations where the stated purpose is to tolerate only the barest hints of capitalism.

Positive Economics
A term indicating economic statements that are purely descriptive (versus normative economics, which is loaded with value judgments).

Positive economics is concerned with explaining how and why we got where we are, and what the outcome of a particular policy is likely to be. It does not concern itself with questions of whether where we are is good or bad, or whether the outcome of a policy is socially desirable or not. For example, in debates over tax policy and income distribution, positive economics will focus on questions of efficiency rather than equity. See NORMATIVE ECONOMICS.

Price System
Way of allocating resources that also transmits information on demand-and-supply conditions. That's the short definition. A longer, more satisfying, explanation requires a play-

by-play account of what happens in an idealized free market where buyers and sellers are free to interact.

Consider the simple island economy so beloved by economists. The scene opens on two sellers, one with bananas and one with oranges. They meet and greet as sellers but quickly turn into buyers when they exchange goods—let's say four bananas are exchanged for two oranges. (Note that prices don't have to be fixed in monetary terms, just in relative value: Two oranges are worth four bananas.) Scene two is a terrible storm which destroys most of the banana crop but leaves the orange crop—which has been harvested and stored —untouched. Scene three takes place a week later, after the banana famine has been felt by the island. This time, when the banana seller and the orange seller meet, they exchange two oranges for one banana. Final curtain.

What has happened? The relative scarcity of bananas has caused their price to rise; that is, bananas will now go to those who prize them enough to pay more oranges for them. And, voilà, the effects of the terrible storm have been transmitted through the price system.

Needless to say, the working of the price system in the real world is not as efficient as it would be in a simple island economy. In the real world, government regulations that set price floors (supports) or price ceilings (controls), and the existence of a certain class of goods known as "public goods," block the price system from the efficient allocation of resources and the transmission of information.

Say, for example, the government of the simple island economy institutes a price support program for oranges; that is, the government decrees that the price of oranges may not fall below two bananas. Thus, the orange seller cannot offload his oranges at the one banana price asked by the banana seller. Instead, the government must stockpile the unsold oranges—hardly an efficient allocation of oranges and certainly a misrepresentation of the supply-and-demand situation. (That, by the way, is how the U.S. farm program, with its complicated system of price supports, works.)

Private Sector
Economic activity—personal and business—excluding the government's contribution.

Privatization
A newly fashionable word to describe the process whereby the government transfers responsibility for delivering certain services to the private sector. The opposite of nationalization. See NATIONALIZATION; PUBLIC GOODS.

Productivity
A widely used term that can mean almost anything.

Even if the term is used precisely—a ratio that measures

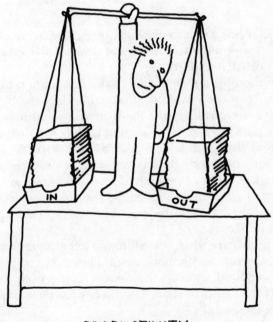

PRODUCTIVITY

how much input produces how much output—its application can be fuzzy. Take the most often used measure of productivity, labor, which is usually expressed as the ratio of output to the number of labor hours spent producing that output. Labor productivity is said to be rising if it takes less time for workers to produce the same amount of output. But what does that really measure? Any number of things: workers are working harder, workers are working smarter, or workers are working with better machines.

At any rate, the measurement of productivity is less important than its result. The more productive an economy is, the better off its members are either because the same amount of goods and services are being produced with less work or more goods and services are being produced with the same amount of work.

Profit

The term seems straightforward enough, and in everyday life it is. But, for economists, the idea of profit is divided into two types—normal and pure.

Normal profits are embodied in the minimum return necessary to keep the factors of production doing what they're doing. It's the earnings that the owner of a business retains after she pays her explicit costs: rent to the owner of the store or factory, the salaries or wages to her workers, and the money for any goods or services she uses to produce her product. The money that's left after explicit costs are paid is then attributed to implicit costs: the return on factors such as the capital she has tied up in her business, and the opportunity cost of her labor.

Pure profits are what, if anything, is left after deducting all the explicit costs and implicit costs. These are returns above what is required to keep the factors doing what they are doing. If normal profits are like cake, then pure profits are like icing on the cake.

There are several ways of looking at profit—other than as theft by greedy, exploitative capitalists. First, profit can be seen as the return for bearing risk. After all, business is subject to failure; profits are the reward for taking a chance. Second, as Schumpeter argued, profit can be seen as the return for innovation. It's both the incentive that motivates entrepreneurs, or innovators, and their reward.

Third, profit can be, simply, a matter of luck. Consider the "windfall gains" captured by owners of oil or housing during the 1970s. And finally, profit can be a return to the owner of a monopoly. Here, monopolies include things like a patent on an invention, an outstanding tenor voice, some acres of land in Bordeaux as well as ownership of the company store in a coal-mining town. See WINDFALL PROFITS.

Protectionism

All-purpose term to describe government efforts to shield the domestic economy from competition from abroad. Protectionism can take many forms: quotas or increased taxes on imports, and/or subsidies and reduced taxes for the home team.

Protectionists like to identify situations that, they argue, merit special consideration. Some industries, like those that feed into national defense and agriculture, are said to have strategic importance for the country's ability to wage war. Other industries, like so-called infant industries, are thought to deserve protection until they have developed a requisite maturity—until they're big enough to fight their own battles. Of course, once they're big enough, or so goes a fourth argument, they become so important for the national economy that they, too, must be protected.

There are, however, many economic problems with protectionism. It violates the notion of comparative advantage which holds that all countries are better off if they produce whatever they are relatively best at producing. It can be ex-

PROTECTIONISM

pensive for consumers who are denied cheaper imports; likewise it can feed inflation because sheltered industries can inflate their prices. And, once protective legislation is in place, it's tough to dismantle. See QUOTA; SUBSIDY; TARIFFS.

Public Goods

Two parts to the definition here: Public goods can be consumed by more than one person and, once having been supplied to one person, cannot be denied to another.

This is an idea that demands concrete illustration: National defense is a public good—all citizens can use it and it is impossible to provide it for you without providing it for me, too. Other examples are public parks, clean air, and streetlights.

The example of choice for economists is lighthouses. While it's certainly true that a ship in a storm-tossed sea benefits from a lighthouse, the shipowner has little incentive to build and operate a lighthouse because, once it is beaming, all ships on the storm-tossed sea can use its signal without paying for it. In other words, while everybody benefits from the service, nobody wishes to underwrite its provision. Thus, it makes sense for the government to step in, build and operate a lighthouse, and either pay for it with general revenues or by taxing all shipowners.

However, solving the problem of who should provide public goods (note how appropriate their first name) only gives way to the next problem—how much of any public good should be provided. The answer is, unfortunately, that absent the free market, with its price signals, the government ends up guessing. Hence there is often inefficiency in the provision of public goods.

Too, some economists argue that the government has mistaken some private goods for public ones. And there are, in fact, lots of examples of public goods that are also provided by the private sector: garbage collection, mail delivery, education, housing, and police protection. Critics want these ser-

PUBLIC GOODS

vices "privatized"; that is, returned to the market so that price signals can ensure more efficiency in the delivery of these services. See PRIVATIZATION.

Public Sector
That part of economic activity that includes federal, state, and local governments, but excludes personal and business activity.

Quantity Theory of Money

A tautology that looks like this: $MV \equiv PQ$, where M is the nation's money supply, V is velocity (how fast money changes hands), P is the price level, and Q is the nation's output.

This tautology is the foundation for monetarism. In its crude form, the V and the Q are just passive, and P responds to changes in M. That is, if the money supply doubles, then prices double.

Sounds simple, and it is. It is also not quite accurate. Historically, changes in the money supply have not caused a one-for-one change in the price level because the two other variables, velocity and output, are not really passive. For example, when velocity falls, prices do not rise as fast as the money supply.

Anyway, a little looseness in the equation doesn't take away from the essential fact that sustained increases in the money supply will, eventually, push up the price level. See MONE-TARISM.

Quasi-Rent

Any extra revenue, after costs have been taken care of, that temporarily accrues to a factor of production. Generally, quasi-rents accrue to factors of production that are scarce for one reason or another.

Say, for example, somebody discovers that unbelievably great bananas can be grown on the island of Manhattan. During the time it takes imitators to pull down skyscrapers and cultivate bananas, the initial grower will reap a quasi-rent from his possession of great banana-growing soil. See RENT.

Quota

A quantitative restriction.

Quotas have three applications. When they are applied to imports, they become part of the nation's protectionist policy (as in the case of the United States slapping quotas on Japanese autos). When they are applied to output they become part of a cartel's machinations (as in the case of OPEC which gives each oil-producing member a limit on the oil it can pull out of the ground). And when they are applied to an industry by the government, they become part of public policy (as in the case of the U.S. farm program).

It really doesn't matter for which of the three reasons quotas are used, the result is always the same—prices go up. In the first case, both the protected industry and the quota-levied foreign industry can raise prices on their products. And in the second and third cases, restricting the amount of available product (supply) pushes prices up.

QUOTA

Radical Economics

School of thought that is critical of mainstream economics—Keynesianism, monetarism, and new classical economics.

It's not a stretch to say that radical economics is anticapitalism. It is concerned with issues like the distribution of income and wealth, rather than with questions relating to economic growth.

Other than ideology, the chief difference between radical and mainstream economics is that the radicals include social and political issues as proper subjects of economic inquiry. They argue that traditional economics has become too focused and mathematical, and thus trivial. For their part, mainstream economists accuse radical economists of possessing too much cant and too little science.

Rational Expectations

A school of thought that describes how people respond to economic events. Dubbed ratex, it is based on the notion that people aren't fooled by government schemes to manipulate their behavior. Briefly, here's the reasoning: Since people have the same access to information that the government does, they can anticipate the government response to that information. Moreover, by anticipating government action, people can render government's policies ineffective.

Consider what happens when the budget deficit becomes alarmingly huge. People know, based on its past actions, that government will try to reduce the deficit by increasing taxes to raise revenue. However, since people act in their own best interest, they will protect themselves from a tax hike (and a fall in their after-tax income) by saving more money. But when they save more, they spend less which, in turn, slows the economy and depresses tax revenues. The net result, then, is that tax policy will be checkmated. The government ends up with less revenue, not more. And, of course, the budget deficit will grow larger.

Hence, ratexians argue that fancy government schemes to

"manage" the economy—that is, to manage people's behavior—are ineffective. Indeed, most ratexians would argue that government intervention in the markets causes confusion and second-guessing and can be downright dangerous. In short, they say that the economy would be better off if the government kept its hands to itself.

Doubtless, ratex represents a twentieth-century version of Adam Smith's argument that free markets create national and economic health more effectively than does government meddling. And doubtless, too, the ratexian notion that people can't be fooled by government policy seems little more than common sense. Nonetheless, ratexian notions seem fresh compared to the orthodoxy of the past twenty years when economists and politicians believed that government intervention in the markets could increase production, decrease unemployment, and control inflation. In the sixties, for instance, Keynesians thought that government could even smooth out the ups and downs known as business cycle fluctuations, and thus put an end to recessions; this was known as fine tuning.

Ratex got its start, slowly, in the sixties. It gained adherents among young economists in the seventies when persistent economic slumps put an end to grandiose notions like fine tuning. In fact, ratexian ideas even began to slip out of university economics departments to affect government policy (the effort to deregulate the economy that began in the Carter administration reflects this new laissez-faire thinking). And some of its adherents are looking to the eighties and nineties for an ideological coup that would end active government involvement in the economy. See KEYNES, JOHN MAYNARD; MONETARISM; NEW CLASSICAL ECONOMICS.

Reaganomics

An economic policy followed by the Reagan administration from 1980 on. The idea was that cutting tax rates on individuals and businesses would encourage them to save and invest;

this increased saving and investment, in turn, would generate higher incomes, more business, and more jobs. Reaganomics further argued that the super economic growth unleashed by the tax cuts would result in more tax revenues—enough to reduce the deficit and even produce a balanced budget.

That was the theory, anyway. The reality depends on who's doing the talking. Nobody disputes the fact that—despite astounding economic growth in 1983–84—the Reagan administration was dogged by truly huge budget deficits. But supporters fix the blame for those shortfalls on the Federal Reserve Board. The Fed, which had become concerned about runaway inflation, started restricting the amount of money in the economy in 1979, and that precipitated a steep recession. That recession, say supporters, ballooned the budget deficits by shrinking personal and corporate tax revenues and swelling government spending on programs like unemployment. Critics of Reaganomics, however, argue that the deficits were the result of too much tax cutting and too much government spending on nonrecession-related things, like defense.

The policy was dubbed Reaganomics because it appeared to be rather unique. True, Reaganomics directly contradicted policies followed by the three preceding administrations, policies that involved higher taxes and resulted in low rates of saving and investment and slow economic growth. Nonetheless, Reaganomics was not really revolutionary. The idea of stimulating the economy through tax cuts was enunciated by Keynes and advocated by his followers during the sixties.

Real
Value adjusted for inflation. What isn't called real is called nominal.

Real appears before words like gross national product, wages, income, and interest rate. "Real wages," for example, measures purchasing power. If the rate of inflation was 5 percent last year, and your wages went up 5 percent, then your purchasing power has stayed the same.

Real Economy
Here, real refers to the goods and services part of the economy as distinct from factor payments, or the money part.

Recession
Informally, any period of time during which economic activity is blah; formally, when the economy has not grown for at least two consecutive quarters.

Recessions can be mild (when they don't last too long and economic activity doesn't fall off too much) or they can be severe (when they last over a year and gross national product takes a dive). When a recession lasts a very long time and economic activity plunges, then it is called a depression. See DEPRESSION.

RECESSION

Regulation

Catchall term for government control or overseeing of various activities in the private sector.

The chief economic justification for regulation—and the usual textbook example—has to do with natural monopolies (situations where it's difficult to introduce competition).

Consider the electric power industry where there are tremendous economies of scale associated with having one single producer and distributor of power. A quick and dirty example: Think about the waste of resources in laying and maintaining two, three, or four sets of power lines.

In this case, the first thing the government does is grant a monopoly to one power authority for a geographic area. But then the government must do a second thing—it must regulate that authority to make sure it doesn't exploit its monopoly position by charging high prices. That task is usually assumed by a regulatory commission. Indeed, the toughest, most important, and most interesting issue for regulatory commissions is how to set prices.

On the one hand, the commission must set prices low enough so that the public isn't gouged; on the other hand, the commission has to set prices high enough to ensure that the utility gets enough revenue to stay in business.

But even if regulatory commissions could hit the price right, the right price in January might be totally wrong by November. An unexpected change in the price of an input, like fuel, or a change in the rate of inflation, can skew the whole cost structure and throw prices out of line. This problem is known as regulatory lag.

And these lags can be wicked. Commissions charged with representing the public interest are like giant ships—they cannot adjust quickly. They must call hearings and listen to endless testimony on all sides of the issue; they must deliberate and consider. Of course, while they're busy fulfilling their responsibilities, economic damage can mount.

Regulation, of course, encompasses more than just natural monopolies. Much, much more. In one fashion or another,

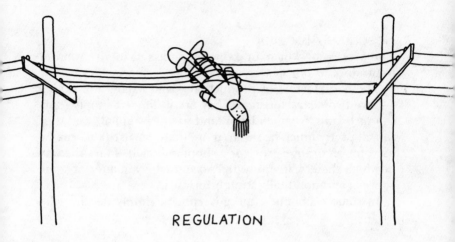

REGULATION

government fools around with almost everything. And, in one fashion or another, the rigidities and inefficiencies associated with regulation impede economic growth.

There are, at any rate, a lot of problems associated with regulation. These problems have led economists to take a new—and severely critical—look at the whole enterprise. And the fresh look has yielded some rather big changes. In some cases, businesses that were thought to be natural monopolies, like telecommunications, have been deregulated. In other cases, regulations that have created cartels, like the airline and trucking industries, have been dismantled. In fact, moves to deregulate the economy have become so commonplace, that deregulation has its own entry. See DEREGULATION.

Rent
The earnings accruing to a factor of production (land, labor, or capital) for which the supply is fixed.

Obviously, economists use the word rent differently than do landlords or tenants. Although land is the classic example of a factor earning rent, a superbly talented chef or an opera diva earns rent, too. See QUASI-RENT.

Resource Allocation

The process by which an economy directs its inputs in order to produce its outputs.

The basic factors of production—land, labor, and capital—have two characteristics. They are in limited supply (only so much land, so much labor, and so much capital), and they can all pretty much be put to more than one use (land can be used for an orange grove or a shopping mall). Thus, the way in which these scarce resources are used is a matter of some concern and not totally straightforward.

In some economies, the government simply decides who

RESOURCE ALLOCATION

gets what resource and for what use. State-planned economies, for example, might direct land, labor, and capital into the production of industrial goods. In other economies, market forces decide who gets what. In a capitalistic economy, for instance, the market might signal that land, labor, and capital will earn their highest return producing consumer goods.

At any rate, economics is generally taken to be the science that studies the intricacies of resource allocation.

Returns to Scale

Term used to describe what happens to a firm's output when its inputs are increased. Returns to scale come in three varieties: increasing, constant, and decreasing.

Increasing returns to scale is what happens when a firm doubles, say, the amount of land, labor, and capital it uses to produce framistans, and, as a result, the amount of framistans it can produce trebles. (The firm has come out ahead.) Constant returns to scale is what happens if a firm doubles its inputs, and its output of framistans then also doubles. (The firm is even-up.) And diminishing returns to scale is what happens when inputs are doubled but output only increases by a half. (The firm should go back to the drawing board.)

RETURNS TO SCALE

Ricardo, David (1772–1823)

An exceedingly influential classical economist (and a fabulously successful stockbroker).

Ricardo is known for *The Principles of Political Economy and Taxation* (1817) which set forth the rather gloomy conditions under which economic growth would eventually stop and wages would fall below subsistence levels. Nobody pays much attention to those arguments anymore; nonetheless, Ricardo's explanation of comparative advantage is still an important idea in international trade. See COMPARATIVE ADVANTAGE.

Ss

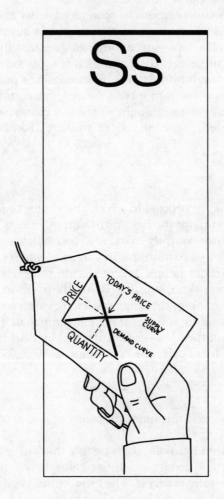

Samuelson, Paul A. (1915–)

Nobel prize–winner in Economics in 1970, for whom no superlative can be said to be an exaggeration.

Samuelson's contributions to economic theory and analysis —particularly to Keynesian economics—are both broad and deep. And surely important enough to give him the kind of stature that can be called towering. But most people know Samuelson through his textbook, *Economics,* first published in 1948. It has brought him lots of money, fame, and—above all—influence. *Economics* taught Keynesian economics to generation after generation of college students. Samuelson has taught at MIT since 1940.

Satisficing

A decision-making process in which the goal is to find a satisfactory solution, not the best, or optimum, one.

Satisficing runs contrary to the microeconomic assumption that firms seek to maximize profits. That is, when faced with a problem, businesspeople might decide that a satisfactory solution is better than one that is strictly profit-maximizing because, for example, the time and energy necessary to discover the best solution is beyond their immediate resources. The word—and the idea—were authored by Herbert Simon, who won the Nobel prize for Economics in 1978.

Savings

Whatever income is not spent on consumption is considered savings.

Thanks to Ben Franklin, most people think of saving as an act of thrift and little else—pennies going into a piggy bank or dollars under the mattress. The economists' view, however, is much more dynamic. Here, saving represents funds available for investment; saving provides funds to replace worn-out capital and to create new forms of capital. That is, saving underwrites the capital stock of the country without which economic growth would come to a halt. Put another, more homely way, if a farmer (society) consumes his seeds (capital) instead of planting them (saving), eventually he will run out of food.

There are three sources of savings in the economy: personal, business, and government. Personal (sometimes called household), is the most familiar type of saving; it's the money that goes into bank accounts or money market funds.

Business saving is less familiar but utterly crucial. Business uses its retained earnings (whatever is not paid out in taxes or dividends) to invest in plant and equipment, or to finance research and development.

As for the government, it hasn't been doing much saving recently—it not only spends whatever it takes in, but then goes out to borrow some more. Nonetheless, the government

SAVINGS

does channel funds into investment goods like highways and bridges.

At the personal level, economists like to distinguish different motives for saving. For instance, people can save for retirement, or against an unexpected occurrence.

As for the exact proportion of income saved, that can be a function of several things. Generally, people with higher incomes save more. (Common sense: Poorer people must spend a higher proportion of their income just to house, clothe, and feed themselves.)

Beyond the level of income, the amount saved can also depend on inflation: The higher the rate, the less incentive to save, since inflation will erode the value of savings. It can also depend on the return to saving; higher interest rates make saving more attractive. Too, tax policy determines incentives to save in the United States; for example, some forms of saving, like Individual Retirement Accounts, are tax-advantaged. And, finally, people who feel that their future prospects are solid will save less than those who are afraid, for example, of losing their jobs.

Say's Law

Named after the French economist, Jean Baptiste Say, who enunciated it in 1803.

Say's Law has been popularly translated into "supply creates its own demand." There are lots of interpretations of Say's law, but the only sensible one is that markets tend toward equilibrium.

Schumpeter, Joseph (1883–1950)

Austrian economist who emigrated to the United States in 1932. Schumpeter wrote about many topics on economics: business cycles, trade cycles, history, and development. He is best known, however, for his work on the importance of entrepreneurs and innovation for economic growth.

Seasonal Adjustment

Fiddling with data that are collected over time.

Consider the statistics on unemployment. Some unemployment is seasonal—there's not much demand for construction workers during the winter, for example. But policymakers, and others, will want to know if a sudden surge in the number of unemployed in December is a natural event or a warning sign that the economy is heading for a recession.

Thus, the figures for unemployment in December will be adjusted—an estimate of how many unemployed are just temporarily jobless construction workers will be subtracted from the total. In other words, eliminating seasonal factors from the data will give a truer picture of the unemployment situation.

SEASONAL ADJUSTMENT

Service Economy

A recently fashionable term used to describe the U.S. economy. Roughly speaking, a service job is anything that isn't a manufacturing job; a secretary working in an auto factory has a service job, while an assembly-line worker in that same factory has a manufacturing job. A service job can be anything from a banker jetting around the world in search of clients to a janitor mopping the basement floor.

The mere existence of the term is a reflection of some broad changes which have been under way during the past three decades. A small but telling example: In 1950, jobs in the service sector accounted for less than half of total employment. Since then, service jobs have grown to somewhere over 75 percent of employment, and the service sector itself accounts for some 70 percent of gross national product.

SERVICE ECONOMY

What happened? Part of the switchover was a natural outgrowth of the expansion of business production through the consolidation of firms. And part was an outgrowth of business expansion from local to national to international reach. Both these developments required an expansion in support services—the communications, transportation, financing, and information processing necessary to keep business flowing along at a reasonable clip.

Another contributing factor was the entry of women into the labor force in the sixties. Once these women left home, they needed to purchase the services that they had been providing "for free." Hence the growth in child care and fast-food services, along with fancier stuff like personal shoppers and financial planners. So, too, the explosion in health services is due to the fact that Americans are living longer and richer, and requiring everything from nursing homes to personal fitness trainers.

Until the 1980–82 recession, an economy that was strong in services but weak in manufacturing was thought to be, somehow, effete. Manufacturing meant industrial might; it was the muscle that built the United States into a world power. But the staying power of jobs and output in the service industry—power that kept generating jobs and income throughout a recession that saw manufacturing take a hosing —has started to reverse that prejudice.

Indeed, a more reasonable view of the service industry is that it can facilitate manufacturing. What good is a yardful of widgets if the widget maker can't use telephones to sell them, trucks, trains, and airplanes to transport them, and computers to keep track of all those activities.

Short Run

Any period of time too short to allow a firm to change or vary all its factors of production.

Say that Framistan International discovers that its orders outpace its productive capacity. And say that it will take

Framistan International two years to expand its production capacity by building a new factory. Then, everything that Framistan does during those two years—like hiring more workers—consists of things done in the short run.

For some economists, short run is any time period where there is a disturbance in equilibrium. Say that the actual price of framistans is above the market price because demand is very strong. Economists would describe that situation as a disequilibrium in the short run because, by definition, equilibrium is what must happen in the long run. See LONG RUN.

Smith, Adam (1723–1790)

A Scottish philosopher and probably the founder of modern economics. In his classic, *The Wealth of Nations* (1776), Smith proposed a major departure from the practice of letting politicians and kings—or queens—fiddle with the market. Indeed, Smith tut-tutted over a seemingly endless amount of follies and fiascos that had resulted from state interference in the economy.

Smith suggested that the way to promote national wealth was to allow individuals to pursue their own economic interests in a free market. The process by which behavior aimed at selfish gain results in the general benefit is described by Smith's enduring metaphor the "invisible hand." Other terms associated with Smith are "economic laissez-faire" and "free enterprise." No accident, then, that the burgeoning bourgeoisie of the next century—and the established bourgeoisie beyond—cleaved to Smith's celebration of their importance to national health and well-being. See INVISIBLE HAND.

Social Benefit; Social Cost

Something that affects everybody, not just specific individuals or firms. A social benefit like clean air improves the welfare of society, while a social cost like pollution detracts from it. Social costs or benefits are often called externalities.

Socialism

An economic (and political) system where most property is publicly, not privately, owned.

Under socialism there is no market in the sense that prices are set by the government. And there is no profit motive in the sense that profits belong to everyone (income is distributed by the government). Economists call socialism a command, or planned, economy because it is necessary for large government bureaucracies to command, or plan, resource allocation. See PLANNED ECONOMY.

Stagflation

Term popular in the 1970s to describe a situation with both high rates of inflation and low, or negative, rates of economic growth.

Stagflation mystifies some economists because, prior to the 1970s, inflation was thought to be the result of red-hot economic growth. Economists assumed that inflation happened when demand outstripped the economy's capacity to produce —certainly not when the economic activity was slack and a lot of workers were unemployed. During the 1970s, however, inflation zoomed while the economy languished and unemployment stayed stubbornly high.

The usual explanation for stagflation says that after a period of high inflation people learn to expect still more inflation. Thus, price increases are built into contracts—like labor agreements—which, in turn, push prices further up.

The policy dilemma here is that if the government tries to slow inflation by clamping down on spending and money growth, the immediate effect is that the economy contracts, slowing the growth of output, but labor and raw material prices will continue to increase. Simply put, government policy will cause a recession without taming inflation. On the other hand, if the government tries to match the growth in wages and costs with expansionary fiscal and monetary policies, it will create more inflation.

Subsidy

Money that is paid by the government to keep goods or services "affordable."

Usually subsidies take the form of payments to the producers. The money paid to producers raises their income above what it would otherwise have been—they are quite literally paid to produce—with the hope that higher production will lower prices. If all goes according to plan, the subsidy is also a subsidy for the consumers, who, of course, pay less than they otherwise would have. Public transit is a favorite form of government subsidy.

Supply

Shorthand expression for the relationship between the willingness to sell something and its price. It's hard to underestimate the importance of supply for economic analysis. Supply and its twin, demand, are the foundations on which modern microeconomics rests.

Supply has a precise, mathematical meaning for economists. And learning that exact meaning requires digesting several chapters in an introductory textbook, chowing down concepts like iso-quants, production functions, variable and fixed costs, and—for the sophisticated—understanding integral calculus. Scholarly application notwithstanding, supply can also be understood in one, commonsense sentence: Producers will offer more of their product when its price rises, and less of it when its price falls.

The relationship between the quantity supplied and its price is best expressed graphically by something called a supply curve. Consider a supply curve showing how many framistans a framistan producer can supply over a year. Possible prices per framistan can be put on the vertical axis (from $1000 to $4000), the number of framistans on the horizontal axis (from zero to 150).

The supply curve consists of plotting how many framistans the producer will supply to the market at each price; say, for example, at \$1000, the producer will supply 50 framistans, and at \$2000, the producer will supply 100. When the points showing how many framistans will be offered at each price are connected by a line, that line will slope upward from left to right. That is, there is a positive relationship between the quantity supplied and the price; as prices rise, quantity increases.

The line's upward direction, what economists call its positive slope, is due to the so-called law of supply. (When properly drawn, the line is actually a curve whose slope depends on the elasticity of supply.)

What's behind the law of supply—other than the notion that people will be willing to offer more of a product the higher its price? For economists, the answer has to do with the cost structure of the firm. Costs come in several guises: There are labor costs, materials costs, equipment costs, capital costs, and so on and so forth. When all these costs are added together, it's possible to figure out the cost of producing one single framistan (or 10,000, for that matter).

Economists focus on something called marginal cost— what it costs to produce an extra unit. When the marginal cost of one more framistan is below its selling price, then it pays to produce that framistan. Why? Because money can be made by selling it. And, of course, if the marginal cost is above the market price, then it doesn't pay to produce more framistans. Simply put, the marginal cost curve—how much extra each additional framistan costs to produce—is the supply curve for the firm. As the prices rise, it pays for a firm to produce more framistans because it can produce farther up on its marginal cost curve. (The more general explanation for the positive slope is the law of diminishing returns—as returns go down, marginal costs go up.)

When all the individual supply curves for framistan producers are added together, the result is a supply curve for the entire framistan industry.

Despite the fact that this explanation seems very precise, almost static, supply curves can be slippery things. Both the market supply curve, as well as the curve for an individual firm, can shift around. Say, for example, the price of raw stanislaws, the chief ingredient in framistans, falls. That will lower the cost of producing framistans (including the marginal cost) so that the whole supply curve will fall—or, as economists say, shift to the right. Thus, instead of the old relationship where, at the $2000 price, 100 framistans will be supplied, now 150 framistans can be offered. See DEMAND; ELASTICITY; MARGINAL ANALYSIS; SUPPLY AND DEMAND.

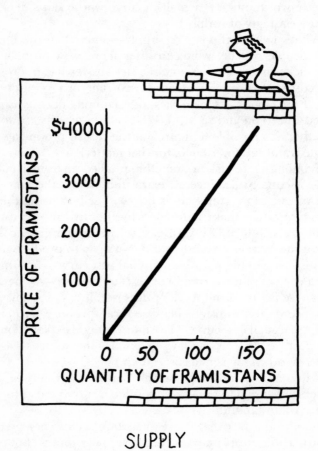

SUPPLY

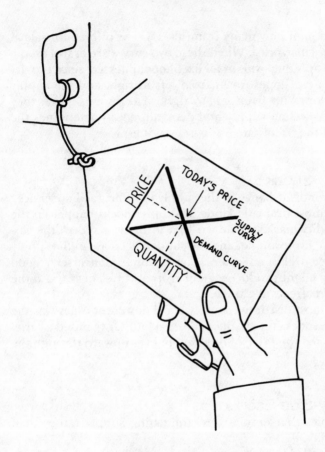

SUPPLY AND DEMAND

Supply and Demand

Term capturing the way prices are set in a free market. This isn't fair, but if you read the Demand and the Supply entries, this one will be a snap to grasp.

Take, on the one hand, the demand curve—that graphical expression of how many framistans will be bought at any particular price. Then take the supply curve—that graphical expression of how many framistans will be offered for sale at any particular price. When these two curves are drawn on the same graph they will, in all likelihood, intersect since the demand curve slopes down from left to right and the supply curve slopes up from left to right. The spot at which they intersect—when supply and demand meet—determines the price of the framistan. See DEMAND, SUPPLY.

Supply Shock

A sudden disturbance in the supply of some good or service.

The most dramatic kinds of supply shocks happen in the commodity markets. Bad weather in Brazil can deck the coffee crop, for example, and the sudden decrease in the supply of coffee will send prices skyrocketing. Conversely, good weather might produce a giant crop of coffee beans, and the price of coffee will plunge.

The most disruptive supply shock in recent times was the oil price shocks that happened when OPEC organized a cartel that caused the price of oil to zoom ever upward through the 1970s.

Supply-Side Economics

Economics that emphasizes stimulating supply rather than demand.

Demand-side economics and the policies that flowed from it were hot during the sixties and seventies. Government concentrated on pumping up the demand for goods and services. That translated into higher and higher taxes so that government could have larger and larger revenues so it could have more and more to spend. The results of these policies, among other things, were high rates of inflation, stubborn budget deficits, and—eventually—low rates of economic growth.

Supply-side economics, which became the rage in the late seventies, takes an entirely opposite approach. Here, government concentrates on increasing supply, or production, through its tax policies. The centerpiece of supply-side economics is the call for cuts in marginal tax rates. It's a simple notion: If you get to keep a larger portion of each extra dollar you earn, you will work more. This incentive effect holds true, too, for saving and investing, since the after-tax return on a dollar saved will go up when the tax rate does down. Thus, supply-side policies are designed to encourage work, saving, and investment.

Further, supply-siders disagree with demand-side orthodoxy over the impact of federal budget deficits. Supply-siders argue that budget deficits, by themselves, are not inflationary; they only become so when the Federal Reserve decides to print money to pay for the borrowing.

While supply-side arguments seem like good common sense, their actual effect is a matter of some dispute. Many economists feel that tax rates in the United States are not high enough to discourage work, saving, and investment; they question whether cutting marginal rates will call forth the productive burst in economic growth claimed by supply-siders. See REAGANOMICS; TAXES.

Tariffs
Taxes imposed on imports.

Tariffs are a favorite tool for protectionists because, unlike quotas and subsidies, they are taxes—they raise revenue for the government. Further, tariffs are perceived as punishment aimed at foreigners; after all, they must pay the tariff.

Nonetheless, tariffs result in the same old protectionist mess. Even though a tariff will cause foreigners to sell less, the tariff becomes embodied in higher prices, regardless of whether the good is foreign-made or domestically produced. Thus, consumers lose (prices go up), producers win (they can raise their prices), the economy suffers (inflationary pressures are created, and diminished competition causes inefficiencies). See PROTECTIONISM; QUOTA; SUBSIDY.

Tax Equity
What designers of tax systems try to achieve.

The notion behind tax equity is that while paying taxes is not pleasant, at least it should be fair. That's easy to say. But there are two aspects to equity—horizontal and vertical. Horizontal means that everybody with the same amount of income should pay the same amount in taxes; vertical means that people with more income should pay more taxes. Unfortunately, under the current income tax system, with its hundreds of loopholes, not only do people with identical incomes pay wildly differing tax bills, but some rich people pay less than some poor people.

Tax Expenditure
Tax laws that lower the tax burden by granting deductions, exemptions, or credits. The reason such legal loopholes are called expenditures is because the government "spends" the revenue by not collecting it in the first place.

Tax Incidence

What befalls the person holding the hot potato when time is called.

Tax burdens can be shifted around. Say you must pay a tax on the bananas you sell. If you simply add it to the price of the bananas, then even though you pay the tax money to the government, the incidence of the tax falls on the buyer.

TAX INCIDENCE

Taxes

No jokes about death and taxes here. Taxes are a serious and complicated matter. Strictly speaking, the purpose of taxing things—earnings or goods or services—is to raise revenue so that the taxing authority can perform certain duties. The taxing authority that looms largest is the federal government. And, presumably, the duties performed by the federal government are commonly agreed-upon functions, from providing for defense and disabled citizens to aiding farmers and small businesses.

Currently, the major tax is one on earnings. Most people pay two types of federal taxes: a straight percent of payroll earnings for the Social Security tax and a progressive percent of earnings for the income tax. "Progressive" means that tax rates increase with income; it is based on the notion that those who can afford to pay more, should.

So far, so good. But now for the complications. The mere existence of a tax distorts economic behavior. A tax tacked on to the price of a bunch of bananas, for example, means the bananas cost more money. All other things being equal—as economists are fond of saying—people would buy fewer taxed bananas than they would untaxed bananas. Thus, a banana tax can be a powerful way to discourage banana buying.

Ditto for a tax on earnings, particularly given the system of marginal tax rates where each extra dollar of income earned is subject to a higher tax rate. People have less incentive to earn that extra dollar because they will have to pay more of it in taxes or, put another way, they will be allowed to keep less of it. This is known as the incentive effect and—brother—it can be wicked.

So wicked, in fact, that some people, faced with high marginal tax rates, reduce their work effort rather than "working for Uncle Sam." Others are driven into what's politely called tax avoidance: At best, they don't declare some portion of their income or, at worst, they don't file any tax return. The increasing number of Americans who avoid taxes, along with the negative impact the incentive effect has on work (and on savings, too) has prompted some observers to call for a different system of taxation. See FLAT TAX; VALUE-ADDED TAX.

Terms of Trade

One of those international terms to describe who is winning and losing in the game of trade.

The phrase itself characterizes the changing export-import relationship between nations in real terms. That is, a country experiencing favorable terms of trade is one where the value of its exports rises; thus, it can buy more imports for the same amount of exports.

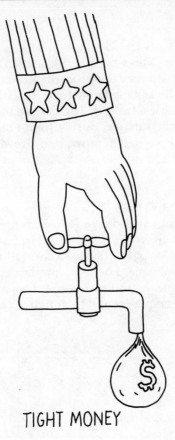

TIGHT MONEY

Tight Money

A completely apt phrase to describe an involved idea. Tight refers to the monetary policy undertaken by the Federal Reserve and money refers to the amount of money in the economy.

When the Fed decides to restrict the availability of credit in the economy, it clamps down on the supply of money. This causes interest rates to rise and borrowing to become unattractive. In other words, tight money means that the Fed has reined in the growth of money.

The opposite of tight money is loose money. See FEDERAL RESERVE SYSTEM; LOOSE MONEY.

Tobin, James (1918–)

Winner of the Nobel prize in Economics in 1981. Tobin has made many outstanding contributions to macroeconomic theory, but he is best known for his defense of Keynesian economic policies. Indeed, Tobin was a member of the Council of Economic Advisers during John F. Kennedy's tenure as president—a veritable festival of Keynesian ideas-put-to-work.

Transfer Payment

A government expenditure for which no service is rendered or product delivered.

Most transfer payments are a form of welfare—Social Security, unemployment benefits, Medicare. The word transfer here really means redistribution. The government collects money from taxpayers and then redistributes it as income.

TRANSFER PAYMENT

Unemployment

The number of workers who aren't working, usually expressed as a percent of the labor force.

Low unemployment—or high employment—is a basic goal of government. Thus, much effort goes into achieving that goal. (The chief platitude is that a fully employed work force makes for healthy economic growth and individual well-being. True. True, too, that a political party that oversees a period of high unemployment usually finds itself unemployed.) Nonetheless, really low unemployment has eluded policymakers in most peacetime years.

There are two kinds of unemployment: frictional and structural. Frictional refers to joblessness that is short term, either because it's seasonal unemployment or because it represents people changing jobs. Thus, stamping out frictional unemployment is impossible and not even desirable.

Structural unemployment refers to joblessness caused by changes in the nature of the economy. The shift out of manufacturing and into services, for example, has caused some structural unemployment. Here, again, stamping out structural unemployment is impossible and not even desirable—an economy that cannot adapt to changes will not be a healthy one.

Beyond these two kinds of unemployment, which set a floor below which unemployment cannot drop, some government policies actually increase joblessness. The minimum-wage law, for example, by setting an above-market wage, means that employers can't afford to hire as many workers as they want. Thus, people who are willing to work for the market wage cannot find jobs. They are involuntarily unemployed. Unemployment compensation, on the other hand, creates voluntary unemployment. Paying people for not working—especially when they are paid more for not working than they would be for working—creates a strong incentive for them to remain jobless.

One final note: For a while policymakers thought they had discovered a trade-off between rates of inflation and the level of unemployment. This relationship, called the Phillips curve, suggested that a high inflation economy would yield low unemployment and vice versa. Unfortunately, however, the relationship has proved a lot more slippery and less sound than it seemed when A. W. H. Phillips published his findings in 1958.

UNEMPLOYMENT

UNION

Union

Organization of workers that—depending on one's bias—either protects its members against exploitation by owners or management, or exploits nonmembers by raising wages above the market price, which, in turn, restricts employment.

No question about it, unions increase individual economic clout. But they do so by limiting the supply of labor. Some craft unions, for example, hold membership down by requiring large initiation fees, long apprenticeships, or strict licensing procedures. And industrial unions bargain for high wages that can make it too expensive for employers to hire additional workers.

Utility

Workpersonlike word to describe the ineffable—the pleasure or fulfillment that people derive from consuming a good or a service.

Utility is a key notion for microeconomics. Because people receive utility from consuming goods and services, they demand goods and services; and because they demand goods and services, goods and services are produced, and so on and so forth.

For the concept of utility to be, well, useful for economists, however, it can't exist in such a nonquantifiable state. Thus, economists invented the "util"—a unit that measures, loosely, satisfaction. Say, for example, you like potatoes twice as much as broccoli; then you can assign 10 utils to the consumption of one pound of potatoes and 5 to a pound of broccoli. To be really precise, however, you must assign these utils over a period of time, say a week or a month. (After all, it makes a difference in your satisfaction if you consume a pound of potatoes in an hour or over a month.)

Consumption decisions are rarely all-or-nothing propositions, but decisions that are made at the margin. Generally you choose between buying more or less potatoes, not whether you should buy any at all. Accordingly, much of economic analysis deals with marginal, or extra, utility. Take, for example, the marginal utility for the consumption of potatoes consumed over a week. Say you derive 10 utils from one pound, 15 utils from two pounds and 18 utils from three pounds, then your marginal utility is 5 from the second pound and 3 from the third pound.

Note that while your total utility is going up, marginal utility is falling. That is due to what economists call diminishing marginal utility; as you increase your consumption of one good, while holding the consumption of all other goods constant, there comes a point where the pleasure you receive from the last unit will decline. (Indeed, if you consumed ten pounds of potatoes in a week, the last potatoes might be totally pleasureless.)

So far, so good. But so far the explanation is missing a crucial ingredient—price. Even if you get twice as many utils from potatoes as from broccoli, you might still buy a pound of broccoli if potatoes are more than twice as expensive as broccoli. Of course: why spend extra money on something that won't give you the full extra pleasure?

Since most people are constrained by limited budgets, consumption decisions are said to be based on marginal utility per dollar. Economists assume that people maximize their satisfaction and pleasure by trying to consume a mixed basket of things such that the marginal utility per dollar of potatoes is equal to the marginal utility per dollar of broccoli, and so on.

Don't, however, be deceived by how orderly all this sounds. As an idea, utility is very slippery, and as an actuality, the utility derived from goods and services for any one person is always changing. See MARGINAL ANALYSIS.

Value Added; Value-Added Tax
The difference between the value of a firm's output and the value of the input purchased in order to produce. It represents, quite literally, the value the firm has added.

The relative simplicity of the arithmetic that goes into figuring value added makes it a juicy target for taxation. Hence, the popularity of a value-added tax, especially in Europe.

A value-added tax is levied at each stage of production. Thus, the farmer who buys seeds and fertilizer pays a tax on the difference between the cost of those raw materials and the value of the wheat she sells to the miller. She will, of course, pass the tax on to the miller by including the tax amount in the price of the wheat. The miller who turns the wheat into flour must pay a tax on the difference between the value of the wheat and the flour, and he, too, will pass the tax on to the baker in his flour prices. The baker, of course, will pass his tax on to his buyer, the supermarket, by including the tax amount in the price of his bread. In the end, it's the consumer who is thought to pay the whole burden of the tax, which will be embodied in the price of the bread at the supermarket's checkout counter.

VALUE - ADDED TAX

Variable Cost
Known informally as operating cost. Any cost that varies with a firm's production. (When a firm isn't producing anything, it's variable cost is zero.) Examples are labor costs, raw materials costs. See FIXED COST.

Welfare State

Exaggerated way of indicating the mechanism by which a mostly market economy fulfills its responsibility to its less fortunate citizens.

In a welfare state, the government assumes the major role in redistributing income from richer to poorer. There are two main mechanisms of redistribution. The state can use its tax revenues to pay for services or goods for the poor, and/or the state can base its system of taxation on the principle that richer citizens should pay more than poorer ones.

A welfare state is not the same as socialism. In a welfare state, the means of production are still, by and large, privately owned.

Windfall Profits

Rather imprecise term to describe any unexpected increase in income received by individuals or firms.

Usually windfall profits accrue to owners of natural resources that are very sensitive to swings in supply-and-demand conditions. A frost on the coffee crop, for example, will produce windfall gains to any plantation owner lucky enough to have escaped the bad weather.

Despite the fact that windfall profits are fortuitous, they seem to create disapproval and, thus, the impulse to tax. Back in the 1970s, for example, the stunning run-up in oil prices led the Carter administration to impose a windfall-profits tax on oil companies. See PROFIT.

World Bank

More formally known as the International Bank for Reconstruction and Development, the World Bank was created in 1944 as part of the forty-five-nation accord reached at Bretton Woods, New Hampshire. The bank's funds come from its member countries (with richer countries making the largest

WINDFALL PROFITS

contributions), from sales of its own bonds, and from earnings on its loan portfolio.

Like any other bank, the World Bank makes loans. Unlike other banks, however, the World Bank is specially charged with making loans to countries that can't get financing from private sources. In practice, that means the bank lends money to a lot of less developed countries for a lot of risky investment projects.

Supporters of the bank argue that poor countries need capital to develop; thus, the bank performs a necessary and useful function. Critics reply that the bank underwrites dubious undertakings that, once created, often need subsidies to operate; thus, the bank leaves debtor countries less able than ever to operate in the world economy.

ZERO-SUM GAME

Zero-Sum Game

An element of game theory where one person's gain is another person's loss. Thus, the winner's gains equal the loser's losses so that the total sum of gains and losses is zero. Less clumsily said: If you get $10 richer, then I must get $10 poorer. The idea has become popular with economists because, it seems, most problems in public policy—like taxation—involve zero-sum solutions. See GAME THEORY.